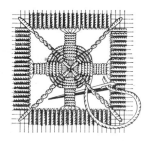

Embroidery

an Illustrated
Teach Yourself book

A sampler, worked in 1789, by Mary Ann Body, aged 9

Jean Kinmond

Illustrated Teach Yourself **Embroidery**

TREASURE PRESS

First published in Great Britain by Brockhampton Press Ltd
(now Hodder & Stoughton Children's Books)

This edition published in 1983 by Treasure Press
59 Grosvenor Street
London W1

© 1972 Hodder and Stoughton Ltd
Revised 1983

ISBN 0 907812 37 6

Printed in Singapore

Line illustrations by courtesy of J. P. Coats (U.K.) Ltd, Paisley.
Photographs on pages 36; 45; 58; 79; 82; 88 supplied by
Coats (U.K.) Ltd, Paisley:
Photographs on page 2 (Sampler); 6 (Nightcap); 9 (Hungarian
Cotton Cover); 34 (Pillow Cover); 49 (Woman's Jacket);
66 (detail of bed-curtain); 67 (Coloured Sampler) and 93
(Child's Smock) reproduced by kind permission of the Trustees of
the Victoria and Albert Museum.

Contents

A man's nightcap embroidered in black silk and
silver gilt thread on linen. English, 16th century

Introduction

Ever since the earliest days of man, embroidery has played an integral part in everyday life. From man's basic needs for shelter, clothing and the storage and transport of food-stuffs, arose the craft of intertwining or weaving fibres and grasses into rough dwellings, coarse fabrics, baskets and containers. The necessity of joining pieces of fabric led to the evolution of a coarse method of stitchery, which in time became the decorative medium which we know as embroidery. Archaeologists have discovered ancient Egyptian baskets constructed from Buttonhole Stitch; Greek embroidery from the fourth century B.C. used Satin, Knot and Chain Stitches, while the Romans regarded embroidery so highly that they called it 'painting with the needle'. Embroidery, using needles made of bone or metal, was an art to be found in places as far apart as China and South America.

As trade developed, so a greater variety of fabrics became available and embroidery grew more elaborate. From the 9th and 10th centuries it was used for Court robes and to enrich church furnishings and vestments. The Crusaders brought home with them from the East rich silks and cloth of gold, from which their banners were made and emblazoned with heraldic embroidery worked by the noble ladies of the household. Elaborate wall hangings, such as the Bayeux Tapestry, which told a story, were apparently fairly common and were certainly worked as a communal project.

With the splendour and pageantry of the sixteenth century, the art of embroidery was developed yet further, encouraged by the ostentatious young nobles of Europe. The contemporary love of flamboyant decoration can be seen in the clothes depicted in portraits of the time, particularly those of Henry VIII and his courtiers, with whom Spanish Blackwork was a particular favourite. Henry's first Queen, Katharine of Aragon, encouraged all things Spanish, including this Spanish style of embroidery which, in its greatly enriched form, became markedly characteristic of Tudor work.

As well as being a fashionable adornment for clothes, embroidery was also much used for furnishings. Trading with China led to the importation of richly-embroidered satins and silks to decorate English homes as bedcovers and wall hangings. As the trend developed, chairs, sofas, screens and even table tops were decorated with embroidery and elaborate canvas work, the styles and designs changing over the centuries, but the embroidery itself always being the work of the lady of the house and her servants. Many great ladies, from Elizabeth I downwards, were celebrated needlewomen.

In complete contrast to the rich luxury of upper class needlework was the peasant embroidery of Europe. Although not worked on velvet and satin, but on locally woven cloths, all styles were equally beautiful, from the gay mid-European Cross Stitch patterns to the fine white embroideries of Scandinavia. These elaborate and traditional embroideries decorated costumes for weddings and holidays, and were worked before marriage on items for the trousseau and the home, the patterns being handed down from mother to daughter. With the spread of communications and the growth of industrial civilization, the traditional peasant forms of embroidery tended to become neglected and it was not until the nineteenth century that there came a revival of interest in peasant traditions. Unscrupulous dealers bought up all the embroidered goods that they could find and it was not until the value of this traditional work was realized by the peasants themselves that a resurgence of interest in the old methods and designs began to be seen again.

The following chapters will show how many traditional styles of embroidery can be adapted to suit today's requirements and how, by using ancient skills, works of real contemporary beauty can be produced.

In this book instructions for working the basic embroidery stitches are given in detail. After mastering these the reader can proceed confidently to the design and techniques of her choice. Some of the more elaborate stitches are also given and the advanced embroideress should find these helpful in creating beautiful work.

A 19th century Hungarian cotton cover, embroidered in long and short stitch, satin and stem stitch

THREAD, NEEDLE AND FABRIC CHART

Fabric	Coats Anchor Embroidery threads	Thickness	Milward International Range needle sizes	Remarks
Fine fabric, lawn, organdie, sheer silk or fine synthetics	Stranded Cotton Pearl Cotton No. 8 Coton à Broder No. 18	1, 2 or 3 strands	Crewel Needles (sharp points) No. Strands 8 1 and 2 strands	These fabrics, threads and needles are for working designs traced or transferred on to the fabric.
Medium weight fabric, rayon, sailcloth, satin, etc.	Stranded Cotton Pearl Cotton No. 8 Coton à Broder No. 18	2, 3 or 4 strands	7 3 strands and Coton à Broder No. 18 6 4 strands and Pearl Cotton No. 8 5 6 strands and Pearl Cotton No. 5	The number of strands of Stranded Cotton may be varied on any article according to the requirements of the design.
Heavy fabric, crash or furnishing fabric	Stranded Cotton Pearl Cotton No. 5	6 strands		
Fine evenweave fabric	Stranded Cotton Pearl Cotton No. 8, 5 Coton à Broder No. 18	1–6 strands	Tapestry Needles (rounded points) No. Strands 1 and 2 strands	These threads and needles are used for working over counted threads of fabric or canvas.
Medium weight evenweave fabric, medium mesh canvas, etc.	Stranded Cotton Pearl Cotton No. 8, 5 Coton à Broder No. 18 Tapisserie Wool	3, 4 or 6 strands	24 3 strands, Coton à Broder No. 18 4 strands and Pearl Cotton No. 8 20 6 strands and Pearl Cotton No. 5 18 |Tapisserie Wool |Soft Embroidery	
Coarse or heavy evenweave fabric, heavy mesh canvas	Stranded Cotton Pearl Cotton No. 5 Tapisserie Wool Soft Embroidery	4 or 6 strands		
Medium weight square weave canvas	Stranded Cotton Pearl Cotton No. 5 Tapisserie Wool Soft Embroidery	3, 4 or 6 strands	Tapestry Needles (rounded points) No. Thickness 20 6 strands and Pearl Cotton No. 5	These threads and needles are used for working over counted threads of fabric or canvas
Heavy square weave canvas	Stranded Cotton Tapisserie Wool Soft Embroidery	6 strands	18 |Tapisserie Wool |Soft Embroidery	
Heavy fabric, crash or furnishing fabric, etc.	Tapisserie Wool Soft Embroidery		Chenille Needle (sharp point) No. Thickness 18 |Tapisserie Wool |Soft Embroidery	These threads and needle are used for traced or transferred design.

Materials

The effective combination of fabric, thread, design and stitch, all carefully chosen for their suitability in relation to each other, can produce work of real beauty, but to achieve this, one must use the best materials.

Needle selection　The chart on page 10 will help the selection of the correct type and size of needle and thread to be used on a variety of fabrics.

Fabric selection　The variety in fabrics is even wider than that of embroidery styles. Choice of fabric is determined by:
1. the type of embroidery to be worked
2. the suitability of the fabric for the article to be made.

In general, most plain fabrics are suitable for free-style embroidery: linen, cotton, and fine wool, as well as the wide range of colourful furnishing fabrics which are available. Choice of fabric is always important and modern furnishing fabrics are very varied in type and texture. They can be shiny or matt, textured or plain, but it is essential to remember that the surface and weight of fabric must be suitable for embroidery stitches.

In certain styles of embroidery, the fabric is characteristic, as in Shadow Work, where a transparent fabric such as organdie is essential in order to achieve the desired effect. Likewise, Hardanger and Drawn Fabric embroidery are traditionally worked on a fine evenweave fabric.

Counted thread embroidery and canvas stitches can be worked on evenweave fabric or a variety of embroidery canvases, all available in varying weights. If a fine effect is desired, choose a fabric with a large number of threads to the inch. If the design is to be bold or is to be enlarged, the fabric must have fewer threads to the inch.

Thread　The type of embroidery thread chosen depends upon the fabric to be worked and the effect desired.

ANCHOR STRANDED COTTON has six separate strands which are loosely twisted together. Six strands may be used at one time, or they may be separated and used singly or in groups of any number. The thread is lustrous and is suitable for most types of embroidery.

ANCHOR PEARL COTTON NO. 5 and NO. 8 is a smooth corded thread most suitable for Hardanger work and other types of counted thread embroidery. Pearl Cotton No. 8 is widely used for Cut-work embroidery. It is also suitable for all medium fine embroidery, both free-style and counted.

ANCHOR TAPISSERIE WOOL is a firm, well-twisted woollen yarn, excellent for canvas embroidery and the working of tapestries, as well as free-style and counted thread embroideries. It is moth resistant and colour fast and can be washed with other threads without any danger of the colour running.

ANCHOR SOFT EMBROIDERY is a thread with a thick, matt finish for bold embroidery in either free-style or counted thread. It is also suitable for tapestries.

Equipment

Needles　In free style embroidery Milward International Range crewel and chenille needles are ideal, the former for fine and medium weight threads and fabrics, the latter for heavier threads and fabrics. For counted thread embroidery Milward International Range round pointed tapestry needles should be used.

(A) Milward International Range tapestry needles No. 18, for Soft Embroidery or Tapisserie Wool (*actual size*)

(B) Milward International Range tapestry needles No. 20, for Stranded Cotton (*actual size*)

Scissors　These should be sharp with finely pointed blades for trimming away the surplus fabric in Cut-Work, as well as for snipping the threads in Hardanger Embroidery.

Thimbles When embroidering it is essential to use a thimble to protect the middle finger when pushing the needle through the fabric. Buy a good quality thimble in metal (preferably silver) or plastic and make sure that it fits well.

Embroidery frames Some embroideries with areas of closely worked stitches are apt to pucker or pull out of shape. In such cases the use of an embroidery frame is recommended to help keep the work flat and even.

There are several types of frame, an embroidery ring being most commonly used for small pieces of work. The ring usually consists of two wooden or metal rings fitting closely, one within the other, so that the fabric may be stretched tightly. These rings can be obtained in various sizes, the most useful type having a small screw on the larger ring for loosening or tightening. This enables any thickness of fabric to be used.

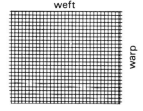

weft / warp

The section of embroidery to be worked is placed over the smaller of the rings, the other ring is pressed down over the fabric on the smaller ring to hold the work taut. If a screw is attached this should be tightened. The fabric must be stretched so that the warp and weft threads remain at right angles to each other and the fabric does not pucker.

For large pieces of embroidery, especially tapestries, the work should be mounted on a square or rectangular frame. These frames generally consist of two rollers, each with a piece of tape firmly nailed along its length (i.e. top and bottom) and two side laths which fit into holes or slots on each roller. The fabric or canvas to be worked is stitched to the tape on each roller. The side laths are then secured with screws to make the fabric taut and even. The sides of the fabric are securely laced round the laths with double cotton thread; if fine fabric is used stitch tape to the free side then lace.

Embroidery rings and frames can be supplied with a stand which leaves both the worker's hands free.

Preparation and care

TRACING METHODS FOR FREE STYLE EMBROIDERY

An embroideress who has created her own design will require to trace it on to the selected fabric. In this book designs are illustrated in such a way that a full-sized drawing can be made and traced on to the fabric. Four methods of tracing are described, the most suitable one being selected for each individual piece of work.

Using carbon paper
1. The simplest method is with the use of carbon paper. Yellow or light blue carbon paper may be used on dark coloured fabric, black or dark blue carbon on light coloured fabric. First, trace the design on to firm tracing paper. Place the carbon paper in position face downwards on the fabric with the drawing or tracing of the design on top. Draw over all the lines with a sharp pointed pencil. Care must be taken to press only on the lines of the design otherwise the carbon may smudge the fabric.

Using tracing paper
2. Trace the design on to firm tracing paper then with a needle prick small holes along all the lines, spacing the holes evenly about 1/16" (2 mms) apart. Rub the back of the pricked design with fine sandpaper to remove the roughness. Place the pricked design on to the fabric and keep in position with weights. Rub powdered charcoal (for light coloured fabric) or powdered chalk (for dark coloured fabric) through the holes. Remove the tracing paper and blow off the surplus powder from the fabric. Paint over the dotted lines of powder with water colour paint using a fine brush and not too much water. Use dark or light coloured paint depending on the colour of the fabric. Alternatively, a fixative spray may be used to fix the powder to the fabric.

Direct tracing
3. A tracing can be made directly on to fine transparent fabric such as organdie, nylon or fine silk by placing the design underneath the fabric and painting over the lines with water colour paint or tracing with a soft pencil.

Stitched tracing 4. On very coarse or textured fabrics the pile may make it difficult to trace or paint a design. In this case, trace the drawing on to fine tracing paper, baste the paper in position on the fabric then carefully follow all the lines of the design with small running stitches. The drawing can be torn away before the embroidery is started and the basting stitches removed after completion of the embroidery.

For hints on enlarging or reducing designs, see page 44.

COUNTED THREAD EMBROIDERY

In contrast to free style embroidery, counted thread embroidery designs require no tracing but are worked by counting the threads of the fabric following a diagram or chart. Each stitch is worked over an exact number of threads. Evenweave fabric or canvas must be used.

STRETCHING FABRIC OR CANVAS

After an article with closely packed stitchery has been worked, the embroideress may find that the fabric has become slightly out of shape owing to the pull of the stitches. This is common in canvas work or tapestry. The fabric or canvas will therefore require stretching. This can be done professionally but the following method can be used quite easily at home. *Note:* There must be a generous surplus margin all round the embroidery so that the area which has to be pinned can be cut away before making up.

1. Cover a firm board or wooden surface slightly larger than the completed piece of fabric or canvas with clean blotting paper 2" (5 cms) larger than the embroidery. Cover this with a sheet of graph paper of identical size. Draw an outline on the graph paper the required size of the finished embroidery plus margin.
2. Pin out the fabric or canvas face downwards to fit the drawn outline. If necessary slightly dampen it. Make sure that the warp and weft threads run exactly at right angles to each other. Secure all outer edges with drawing

pins placed ¼″ (7 mms) apart. The fabric or canvas may require careful pulling in order to make it square.

3. Dampen the back of the embroidery and the surrounding fabric. In the case of canvas, this loosens the gum or stiffening agent and it is possible to stretch the threads back to the original form. The gum or stiffening agent then dries and re-sets the canvas threads. The fabric can be unpinned when dry. However, canvas must be left for two or three weeks so that the shape becomes permanent.

4. Carefully remove pins.

5. If the canvas has been very badly pulled out of shape it may be necessary to repeat the above process.

LAUNDRY

For all embroidery use warm water and pure soap flakes. Wash by squeezing gently. Rinse thoroughly in warm water, squeeze by hand and leave until half dry. Iron on reverse side whilst still damp using a moderately hot iron. An article worked on canvas must be dry cleaned.

ADDITIONAL HINTS

To keep a hem straight

A hem can be kept straight on a coarsely woven fabric by following along a single thread of the material.

To prevent fraying

In working on a material which frays easily, oversew the raw edges before beginning the embroidery.

To correct puckering

Correct slight puckering by 'shrinking'. Damp the work on the wrong side and press with a hot iron over a cloth.

Keeping things tidy

Finally, always keep threads tidy and unravel any knots and tangles before starting work.

Embroidery stitches

In order to carry out the designs shown throughout the book, it is necessary to have a basic knowledge of all the stitches required.

There are some types of embroidery which have an individual style owing to the use of certain characteristic techniques and stitches. Drawn Fabric, Hardanger and Canvas Embroidery come into this category and are all fully described in this book.

Some embroidery stitches are used only in Free Style Embroidery and others are used only in Counted Thread Embroidery, but in certain cases the same may be used for both types of work. For example, one of the Counted Thread stitches (Whipped Back Stitch) can be used over the traced lines of a free style embroidery design, and in the same way certain free style embroidery stitches such as Chevron Stitch, Fly Stitch and Satin Stitch can be used in Counted Thread work.

Back Stitch

Bring the thread through on the stitch line, then take a small backward stitch through the fabric. Bring the needle through again a little in front of the first stitch, take another stitch, inserting the needle at the point where it first came through.

Blanket Stitch and Buttonhole Stitch

These stitches are worked in the same way – the difference being that in Buttonhole Stitch (2), the stitches are close together. Bring the thread out on the lower line, insert the needle in position in the upper line, taking a straight downward stitch with the thread under the needle point. Pull up the stitch to form a loop and repeat.

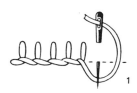

1

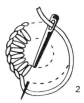

2

Chain Stitch

Bring the thread out at top of line and hold down with left thumb. Insert the needle where it last emerged and bring the point out a short distance away. Pull the thread through, keeping the working thread under the needle point.

Chevron Stitch

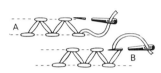

Bring the thread through on the lower line at the left side, insert the needle a little to the right on the same line and take a small stitch to the left emerging half-way between the stitch being made. Next, insert the needle on the upper line a little to the right and take a small stitch to the left as at A. Insert the needle again on the same line a little to the right and take a small stitch to the left, emerging at centre as at B. Work in this way alternately on the upper and lower lines.

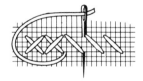

Cross Stitch

Bring the needle out at the lower right-hand side, insert the needle four threads up and four threads to the left and bring out four threads down, thus forming a half cross stitch, continue in this way to the end of the row. Complete the other half of the cross as shown. Cross Stitch may be worked either from left to right, as shown, or from right to left. It is important that the upper half of all the stitches lie in one direction.

Couching

Lay a thread along the line of the design and, with another thread, tie it down at even intervals with a small stitch into the fabric. The tying stitch can be of contrasting colour.

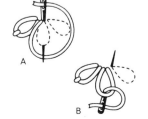

Daisy Stitch or Detached Chain Stitch

Work in the same way as Chain Stitch (A), but fasten each loop at the foot with a small stitch (B). This stitch may be worked singly or in groups to form flower petals.

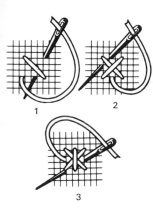

Double Cross Stitch

1 – work a single Cross Stitch; then bring the needle out four threads down and two threads to the left. 2 – insert the needle four threads up and bring out two threads to the left and two threads down. 3 – insert the needle four threads to the right and bring out two threads down and four threads to the left in readiness to commence the next stitch or finish off at the back for a single Double Cross Stitch.

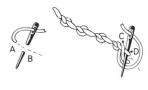

Double Knot Stitch

Bring the thread through at A. Take a small stitch across the line at B. Pass the needle downwards under the surface stitch just made, without piercing the fabric, as at C. With the thread under the needle, pass the needle again under the first stitch at D. Pull the thread through to form a knot. The knots should be spaced evenly and closely to obtain a beaded effect.

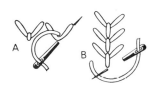

Fly Stitch

Bring the thread through at the top left, hold it down with the left thumb, insert the needle to the right on the same level, a little distance from where the thread first emerged and take a small stitch downwards to the centre with the thread below the needle. Pull through and insert the needle again below the stitch at the centre (A) and bring it through in position for the next stitch. This stitch may be worked singly or in horizontal rows (A) or vertically (B).

Four-Sided Stitch

This stitch is worked from right to left: 1 – bring the thread through at the arrow; insert the needle at A (four threads up), bring it through at B (four threads down and four to the left); 2 – insert at the arrow, bring out at C (four threads up and four threads to the left of A); 3 – insert again at A and bring out at B. Continue in this way to the end of the row or close the end for a single Four-sided Stitch. For Filling Stitch: 4 – turn the fabric round for next and all following rows and work in the same way. Pull all stitches firmly.

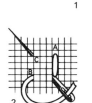

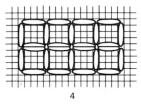

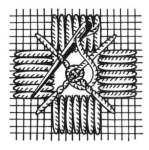

Four-Sided Filling Stitch

Work twisted bars by carrying a thread diagonally across the space as shown, entering the fabric in opposite corner. Twist the thread four times over the diagonal thread back to the starting point. Work a second thread in the same way, but twisting the thread only as far as the centre. Pass the thread over and under the bars twice at centre, then twice over remaining half of second bar to complete.

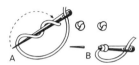

French Knots

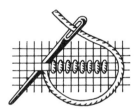

Bring the thread out at the required position, hold the thread down with the left thumb and encircle the thread twice with the needles as at A. Still holding the thread firmly, twist the needle back to the starting point and insert it close to where the thread first emerged (see arrow). Pull thread through to the back and secure for a single French Knot or pass on to the position of the next stitch as at B.

Gobelin Stitch

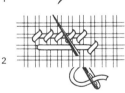

This is a stitch worked over two horizontal threads of canvas and may be worked from right to left or left to right.

Gros Point Stitch

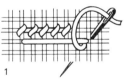

1. Work a Split Trammed Stitch (*see* page 22) from left to right, then pull the needle through and insert again up and over the crossed threads. 2. Pull the needle through on the lower line two double threads (vertical) to the left ready for the next stitch.

Working Gros Point Stitch using both hands. With right hand on top of canvas, insert the needle downwards through the canvas and pull the needle through with the left hand. With left hand, push the needle upwards through the canvas and pull out with the right hand.

Herringbone Stitch

Bring the needle out on the lower line at the left side and insert on the upper line a little to the right, taking a small stitch to the left with the thread below the needle. Next, insert the needle on the lower line a little to the right and take a small stitch to the left with the thread above the needle. These two movements are worked throughout. The

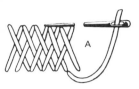

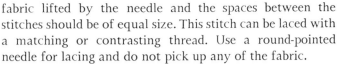

fabric lifted by the needle and the spaces between the stitches should be of equal size. This stitch can be laced with a matching or contrasting thread. Use a round-pointed needle for lacing and do not pick up any of the fabric.

Closed Herringbone Stitch is used for Shadow work. A. shows the stitch worked on the wrong side of the fabric. B. shows the reverse side (that is, the right side of the fabric). The dotted lines indicate the Closed Herringbone Stitch underneath, which shows through the fine fabric.

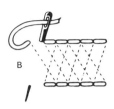

Overcast Bars

To work the Overcast Bars, withdraw the number of threads required from the fabric and separate the loose threads into bars by overcasting firmly over these threads as many times as required to cover the group of threads completely.

Petit Point Stitch

1. Bring the thread out on the left-hand side of the fabric on the top part of the first stitch; pass the needle down diagonally over the crossed threads, then under two threads,

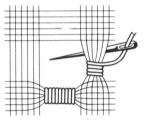

continue in this way to complete the row. 2. The second row is worked from right to left, the needle passing the crossed threads up and over, then under two threads. Work backwards and forwards in this way until the design is complete. All stitches should slope in the same direction.

Ribbed Wheel

Work the Overcast Bars, then work the four Twisted Bars diagonally across the spaces. The centre is formed by taking a Back Stitch over each Twisted and Overcast Bar. Continue in this way until the wheel reaches the desired size.

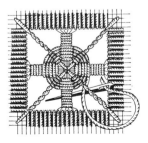

Running Stitch

Pass the needle over and under the fabric, making the upper stitches of equal length. The under stitches should also be equal, but half the size or less of the upper stitches.

Satin Stitch

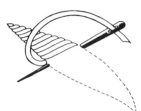

Proceed with Straight Stitches worked closely together across the shape, as shown in the diagram. Running Stitch or Chain Stitch may be worked first to form a padding underneath, this gives a raised effect. Care must be taken to keep a good edge. Do not make the stitches too long, as they would then be liable to be pulled out of position. This stitch may be worked from right to left or left to right. The number of threads over which the stitches are worked may vary, depending upon the effect desired.

Satin Stitch Blocks

This stitch may be worked from right to left or from left to right. The number of threads over which the stitches are worked may vary, depending upon the effect desired.

Seeding

This simple filling stitch is composed of small Straight Stitches of equal length placed at random over the surface, as shown on the diagram.

Smocking Stitches

These are fully described on pages 64–66.

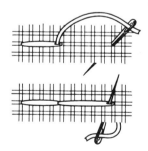

Split Trammed Stitch

Over this horizontal stitch of irregular length, Gros Point is worked (page 20), giving a rich appearance and ensuring better wearing qualities. Split trammed stitches should not overlap. Avoid this by making a split stitch (see diagram)

Stem Stitch

Work from left to right, taking regular, slightly slanting stitches along the line of the design. The thread always emerges on the left side of the previous stitch. This stitch is used for flower stems, outlines, etc. and as a filling.

Straight Stitch

This is shown as single spaced stitches worked either in a regular or irregular manner. Sometimes the stitches are of varying size. The stitches should be neither too long nor too loose. It is also known as Single Satin Stitch.

Twisted Chain Stitch

Commence as for ordinary Chain Stitch, but instead of inserting the needle into the place from where it emerged, insert it close to the last loop and take a small slanting stitch, coming out on the line of the design. Pull the thread through. The loops of this stitch should be worked closely together to have the correct effect.

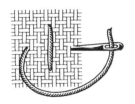

Upright Cross Stitch

The stitches are worked individually. Bring the needle through on the lower point of the cross and insert at the top, taking a stitch through the fabric to one end of the other half of the cross and making a horizontal stitch to complete the cross. It is important that all crosses lie in the same direction.

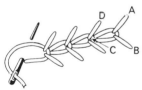

Wheatear Stitch

Work two Straight Stitches at A and B. Bring the thread through below these stitches at C and pass the needle under the two Straight Stitches without entering the fabric. Insert the needle at C and bring it through at D.

Whipped Back Stitch

This stitch is worked from right to left and is used for outlining a design. Work Back Stitch first, then with another thread in the needle, whip over each Back Stitch without entering the fabric.

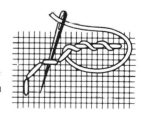

Woven Bars

To work Woven Bars, withdraw an even number of threads from the fabric and separate the loose threads into bars by weaving over and under an even number of threads until the threads are completely covered.

Zig-Zag Chain Stitch

Bring the thread through at (A) and hold it down with the left thumb. Insert the needle at (A) and bring it through at (B), the required length of the stitch. The second stitch is worked in exactly the same way at right angles to the first stitch, but the needle, as it enters the fabric (C) pierces the end of the first loop, thus ensuring that each loop is secured in position.

FURTHER EMBROIDERY STITCHES

Bokhara Couching

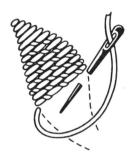

This stitch is worked in the same way as Rumanian Stitch, (see page 27) but the small tying stitches are set at regular intervals over the laid thread to form pattern lines across the shape. The tying stitches should be pulled tight, leaving the laid thread slightly loose between.

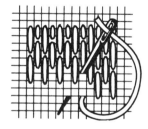

Brick Stitch

This stitch is worked in rows alternately from left to right. The first row consists of long and short stitches into which are fitted rows of even Satin Stitches, thus giving a 'brick' formation. The whole filling must be worked very regularly, making each Satin Stitch of even length and all exactly parallel.

Buttonhole Stitch Bars and Double Buttonhole Stitch Bars

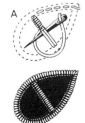

Make a row of Running Stitch between the double lines of the design as a padding for the Buttonhole Stitch. Where a single line occurs, take a thread across the space and back, securing with a small stitch and Buttonhole Stitch closely over the loose threads without picking up any of the fabric (A). Buttonhole Stitch round the shape, keeping the looped edge of the stitch to the inside, then cut away the fabric from behind the bar and round the inside of the shape. Where a double line or a broad bar is required between shapes or sometimes for stems of flowers, when the fabric

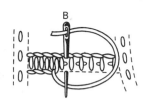

is to be cut away on each side, make a row of Running Stitch along the centre, then Buttonhole Stitch along one side, spacing the stitches slightly. Buttonhole Stitch along the other side into the spaces left by the first row. The fabric is then cut away close to the Buttonhole Stitch, leaving a strong broad bar (B).

Cretan Stitch

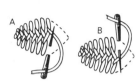

Bring needle through centrally at left-hand side, taking a small stitch on lower line, needle pointing inwards and with thread under the needle point, as shown at A. Take a stitch on upper line, thread under as shown at B. Continue in this way until shape is filled.

Fishbone Stitch

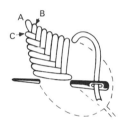

Bring the thread through at A and make a small straight stitch along the centre line of the shape. Bring the thread through again at B and make a sloping stitch across the central line at the base of first stitch. Bring the thread through at C and make a similar sloping stitch to overlap the previous stitch. Continue working alternately on each side until the shape is filled.

Florentine Stitch

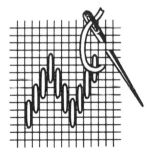

This stitch, generally used to fill a large area, is worked in two or more rows of different colours forming an all-over wave pattern. The size of the wave may be varied, depending upon the number of stitches or the number of threads over which the stitches are worked. The diagram shows the method of working the stitch.

Hemstitch

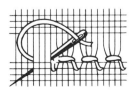

Measure required depth of hem, plus the turnings, and withdraw required number of threads. Do not withdraw the threads right across fabric, but only to form a square or rectangle. Cut threads at the centre and withdraw gradually outwards on each side to within the hem measurement, leaving a sufficient length of thread at corners in order to darn the ends invisibly. Turn back the hem to the space of the drawn threads, mitre corners and baste. Bring the working thread out two threads down from the space of drawn threads through the folded hem at right-hand side, pass needle behind four loose threads, pass the needle over the same four threads and under the fabric, bringing needle out two threads down through all the folds of the hem in readiness for next stitch.

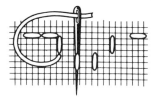

Holbein Stitch

Sometimes called Double Running Stitch. Working from right to left, work a row of Running Stitch over and under three threads of fabric, following the shape of the design. On the return journey, work in the same way from left to right, filling in the spaces left in the first row.

Interlacing Stitch

The foundation of this border stitch is a double row of Herringbone Stitch worked in two journeys, with the stitches intertwined. The first row of Herringbone Stitch is shown in medium tone on the diagram. In working the rows of Herringbone Stitch for the interlacing, there is a slight change in the usual method. In the top stitch the needle is passed under the working thread in each case instead of over, and attention should be paid to the alternate crossing of the threads when working the second row. Do not work this foundation tightly, as the interlacing thread

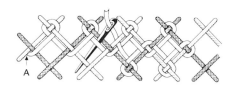

tends to draw the stitches together. When the rows of Herringbone Stitch are worked, bring the thread for the surface interlacing through at A and follow the diagram closely. When the end of the row is reached, lace the thread round the last cross in the centre and work back in a similar fashion along the lower half of the foundation. The last two crosses on the diagram have been left unlaced so that the construction of the Herringbone Stitch may be seen clearly.

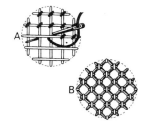

Jacobean Couching or Trellis

This stitch consists of long evenly spaced stitches (Laid Threads) taken across the space horizontally and vertically (A) or diagonally (B); then the crossed threads are tied down at all intersecting points. The tying or couching stitch can be a small slanting stitch or Cross Stitch.

Long and Short Stitches

This form of Satin Stitch is used to fill a shape which is too large or too irregular to be covered by Satin Stitch. It is also used to achieve a shaded effect. In the first row the stitches are alternately long and short and closely follow the outline of the shape. The stitches in the following rows are worked to achieve a smooth appearance. The diagram shows how a shaded effect may be obtained.

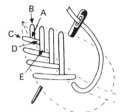

Open Fishbone Stitch

Bring the thread through at A and make a sloping stitch to B. Bring the thread through again at C and make another sloping stitch to D. Bring the thread through at E, continue in this way until the shape is filled.

Pekinese Stitch

Work Back Stitch in usual way, then interlace with a thread to tone or thread of a different colour. The stitch is shown open in the diagram but the loops should be pulled slightly when working.

Raised Chain Band

Work the required number of foundation bars which are fairly closely spaced horizontal Straight Stitches. Bring the thread through at A, then pass the needle upwards under the centre of the first bar and to the left of A. With the thread under the needle, pass the needle downwards to the right of A and pull up the chain loop thus formed.

Rumanian Stitch

A. Bring the thread through at the top left of the shape, carry the thread across and take a stitch on the right side of the shape with the thread below the needle. B. Take a stitch at left side, thread above needle. These two movements are worked until the shape is filled. Keep the stitches close together. The size of the centre crossing stitch can be varied to make a longer oblique stitch or a small straight stitch.

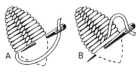

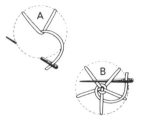

Sheaf Stitch

This filling stitch consists of three vertical Satin Stitches tied across the centre with two horizontal Overcasting Stitches. The Overcasting Stitches are worked round the Satin Stitches; the needle only entering the fabric to pass on to the next sheaf.

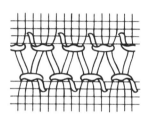

Spider's Web Filling

Commence with a Fly Stitch to the centre of the circle as shown in A, then work two Straight Stitches, one on each side of the Fly Stitch tail, into the centre of the circle. This divides the circle into five equal sections and the 'spokes' form the foundation of the web. Weave over and under the 'spokes' until the circle is filled as at B.

Zig-Zag Hem Stitch

This is worked in the same way as Hemstitch, but there must be an even number of threads in each group of loose threads caught together in the first row. In the second row, the groups are divided in half, so that each group is composed of half the number of threads from one group and half from the adjacent group. A half group starts and ends the second row.

Dictionaries

100 Embroidery Stitches
J. & P. Coats (U.K.) Ltd., Paisley.

Dictionary of Embroidery Stitches. MARY THOMAS
Hodder and Stoughton Ltd, London

Appliqué work

Appliqué or Applied Work is the embroidery technique where a fabric shape, contrasting in colour and sometimes in texture, is applied to another piece of fabric and sewn in position with or without decorative stitches. No other style of embroidery can be so boldly decorative – yet it is simple to do and a dramatic effect can be achieved with speed. It is the perfect medium for free expression in design, as there is no limit to subject, fabric or stitchery. Modern designs rich in colour, shape and texture can be produced by the inexperienced with speed and great enjoyment.

The appliqué shapes must be selected with care and should not be too elaborate. Once they are sewn to the foundation fabric, the decorative embroidery stitches can be planned. The chair pad (page 33) is a simple example of appliqué, enriched with surface stitchery.

The choice of fabric is wide. However, if the embroidery is to be washed, both background fabric and appliqué shapes must be washable and colour fast. The appliqué shapes are sewn in position with a matching sewing thread, Coats Drima. Anchor Stranded Cotton, Pearl Cotton No. 8, Soft Embroidery or Tapisserie Wool may be used for the decorative stitchery, the choice depending upon the final effect desired.

CHAIR PAD

Materials required Coats Anchor Stranded Cotton: 2 skeins Jade 0188; 1 skein each Cobalt Blue 0132, Parrot Green 0255 and White 0402. Use 2 strands for Straight Stitch Stars and Chain Stitch on appliqué shapes; 3 strands for remainder of embroidery.

½ yd (45·7 cms) textured cotton or sailcloth 36 in. (91·4 cms) wide, or other suitable blue cotton fabric.

⅜ yd (34·3 cms) white cotton 36 in. (91·4 cms) wide.

2 yd (182·8 cms) cushion cord to match.

1 reel each Coats Drima (polyester) thread in white and blue.

1 each Milward International Range crewel needles Nos. 7 and 8 (for 3 strands and 2 strands Stranded Cotton respectively).

Details of fish shapes, tails, fins, etc.

To make an oval shape, fold a piece of stiff paper in half and on one side draw a line indicating the size and shape desired. With paper still folded cut round the line and open out flat

A. Five fish body shapes and linking motif
B. Nine fish tails
C. Four fish fins

Instructions Cut blue fabric in half (2 pieces 18 in. (45·7 cms) square). The diagram on pages 30–1 gives shapes for fish body, tail and fins and a circular motif used for linking up the design. Trace the fish shapes and appropriate fins and tails on to blue fabric, and fish shapes only on to white cotton fabric; cut out fish shapes allowing sufficient material round each shape for turnings. Fold in turnings to wrong side and baste with small running stitches. To keep edge of shape smooth and accurate, turnings may have to be snipped at frequent intervals. Place each fish shape in its outlined position on blue fabric and baste in position. Hem round each shape to secure. Follow diagram and number key for embroidery. All parts similar to numbered parts are worked in same colour and stitch.

Make a paper template to required shape of cushion and to size of chair seat. If this exceeds 18 in. (45·7 cms) at widest point, more material will be needed than is specified on p. 29. Place template centrally on two pieces of fabric and trim both to same size. With right sides together, machine round ½ in. (1·2 cms) from edge, leaving opening at back wide enough to allow cushion pad to be inserted easily. Press, trim and overcast seams. Turn to right side.

Working diagram

1 – 0188	2 – 0402	Stem Stitch
3 – 0255	4 – 0188	
5 – 0132	6 – 0402	Back Stitch
7 – 0255	8 – 0188	
9 – 0132	10 – 0402	Chain Stitch
11 – 0188	12 – 0132	Twisted Chain Stitch
13 – 0255	14 – 0188	Herringbone Stitch
15 – 0255	16 – 0188	
17 – 0132	18 – 0402	Straight Stitch
19 – 0188	20 – 0132	
21 – 0255		Double Cross Stitch
22 – 0255	23 – 0188	Upright Cross Stitch

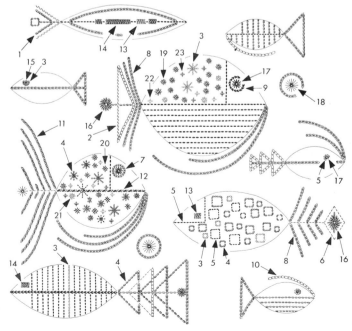

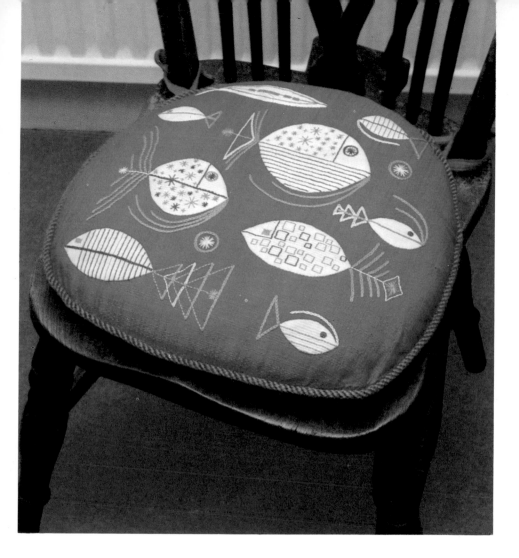

This appliquéd chair seat, making use of fish shapes, adds gaiety to a plain wooden chair and can be adapted for use with an existing chair pad

Make two ties from fabric and attach at each end of opening. Slipstitch cord neatly to edge and insert pad. Turn in seam allowance at opening and slipstitch together. Snap fasteners or a zip fastener may be used to secure opening if preferred.

Blackwork embroidery

Blackwork Embroidery is one of the most popular of the counted thread embroidery techniques. It is frequently termed 'Spanish Blackwork' as it became fashionable in England when Katharine of Aragon was Henry VIII's queen. Later, during the reign of Elizabeth I, it was much used as a dress decoration and also as an embellishment for bed hangings and other household articles.

Originally this style of embroidery was based on the floral forms found in the architecture and decoration of mediaeval Spain and was in effect a copy in miniature of Spanish-Moresque motifs. The early embroideries were traditionally worked on fine white fabric with black or red silk, the outline shapes being filled with geometric stitch patterns. Simple natural forms such as leaves, flowers and fruit can form the basis of a modern design.

Today, the accent is on colour and modern 'blackwork' may be interpreted with coloured fabrics and coloured threads. The choice of fabric is, however, very important as blackwork requires the accurate counting of warp and weft threads. Therefore, the fabric must be evenly woven

This pillow cover is a beautiful example of Elizabethan blackwork

A. The stitches are worked over two fabric threads. The heavy latticed outline is created by using Four-sided Stitch with Cross Stitch centres. The large area within is then intersected by Back Stitches.

B. This lacy filling is composed of Back Stitch, Four-sided Stitch and Cross Stitch, which together form individual 'flower' shapes; these are then connected by a Four-sided Stitch with Cross Stitch centre to form an allover pattern.

C. A honeycomb effect has been created by using Back Stitch over two threads to form octagonal shapes. The 'spot' in the centre of each is formed by a Four-sided Stitch with Cross Stitch centre. The natural square formed between the octagons has been filled with a single diagonal Straight Stitch.

D. In this case, a stitch formation similar to C has been achieved by using rows of individual Ringed Back Stitch connected by perpendicular and horizontal Straight Stitches.

A

B

C

D

with the same number of threads to 1 in. (2·5 cms) in both warp and weft. The most suitable embroidery threads are Anchor Stranded Cotton and Pearl Cotton No. 8.

WORKBAG *Illustrated overleaf*

The simple charm of this workbag is achieved by choosing large leaf, berries and acorn motif and using it as shown in the illustration to form an attractive pattern. The Whipped Back Stitch outline of the motif is shown on the diagram. In the illustration, the filling stitches used in the leaf motifs are those shown in the close-ups above. The berry motif and acorn fillings are worked as shown in the diagram on page 38. Other combinations of filling stitches may be substituted for those shown on the workbag. The colour of the fabric and the thread may be selected by the embroiderer.

Materials required
Coats Anchor Stranded Cotton: 8 skeins Indigo 0127. Use 2 strands for Whipping, 3 strands for remainder of embroidery.

⅝ yd (57 cms) red, medium weight evenweave fabric, 21 threads to 1 in. (2·5 cms), 59 in. (149·7 cms) wide.

⅝ yd (57 cms) dark blue poplin or cotton 36 in. (91·4 cms) wide for lining.

2 wooden handles approximately 13 in. (33 cms) in length.

1 Milward International Range tapestry needle No. 24.

The finished size of the workbag is approximately 13 in. (33 cms) deep and 18½ in. (47 cms) broad. This can, of course, be varied to suit individual requirements.

Positioning Cut a piece from red fabric 20 in. × 31 in. (50·7 cms × 78·7 cms). Mark the centre both ways with a line of basting stitches. The diagram gives one complete motif A, and position of the motif when repeated to left and right hand side. The centre lengthwise basting stitches are indicated by a black arrow. The diagram also gives three leaf sections B, C and D showing the different fillings used; these sections correspond with the shaded areas on the layout. The diagram also shows the arrangement of the stitches on the threads of the fabric represented by the background lines. The layout shows the arrangement of the motifs, the dotted line indicating the centre.

Instructions

With narrow end of fabric facing, commence the design at blank arrow 4½ in. (11·4 cms) down and 1 thread to the right of the crossed basting stitches. Follow the working diagram A and number key for the design and stitches used, and the layout diagram for placing the motifs. The Whipped Back Stitch outlines must be worked first. Fillings A, B, C or D may be worked in the leaf shapes or as indicated on the diagram. Press embroidery on wrong side.

To make up, fold fabric in half widthwise, right sides together and machine stitch each short side to within 6 in. (15·2 cms) of cut edge. Turn to right side. Cut one piece from lining 20 in. × 28 in. (50·7 cms × 71 cms), fold as before and machine stitch short sides to within 4½ in. (11·4 cms) from top edge. Place lining inside bag. Turn in ½ in. (1·3 cms) seam allowance on open side edges of bag and lining and slipstitch close to edge. Attach handles by placing hem allowance through slots, pleating to fit. Turn in ¼ in. (6 mms) and slipstitch securely to lining fabric.

Layout

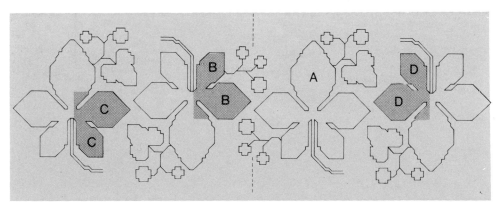

Working diagram

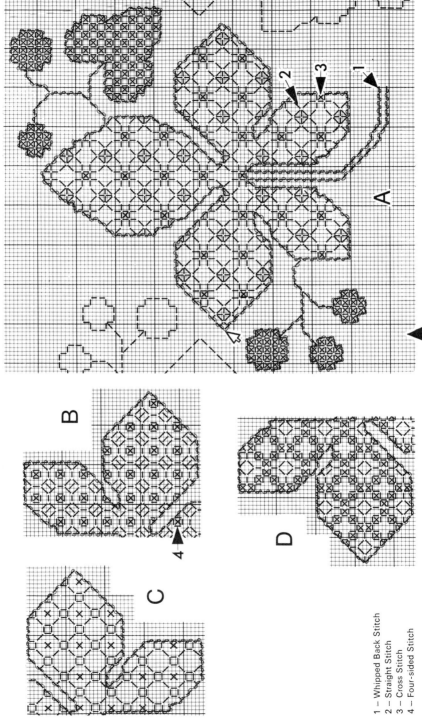

1 – Whipped Back Stitch
2 – Straight Stitch
3 – Cross Stitch
4 – Four-sided Stitch

Cross Stitch embroidery

Cross Stitch is by far the easiest of all embroideries, only one stitch being used throughout – a simple stitch in the shape of a diagonal cross.

It is said that the earliest Cross Stitch patterns originated centuries ago in Russia and further beautiful designs were developed in other Eastern European countries such as Rumania, Hungary, Yugoslavia and Czechoslovakia. In these countries, the tradition was to decorate garments and household linen with this style of embroidery. Many designs were rich in pattern and colour; some had been handed down from mother to daughter and were worked without pattern or chart. In certain cases, individual districts retained their own particular styles.

In eighteenth-century England, chair seats and chair backs were embroidered with Cross Stitch, and during the Victorian period, Cross Stitch was used widely by children to make little pictures and samplers.

Cross Stitch can be suitably used on almost any article – garments and household linen of all types, including curtains, cushions, tablecloths and mats.

The most suitable fabrics are of evenweave, i.e. with the same number of warp and weft threads to the square inch. The fabric should not be too fine, so that counting the threads is easy. Practically any embroidery thread may be used – Anchor Stranded Cotton, Pearl Cotton No. 8, Soft Embroidery and Tapisserie Wool; the choice of thread depending upon the weight and type of fabric and the effect desired.

Cross Stitch can also be worked most successfully on gingham, where each stitch is worked over a check or square. The checks must be suitable in size to the scale of the Cross Stitch embroidery.

One point to remember, even though this stitch is simple, it must always be worked regularly with an even tension and with all the top threads slanting in the same direction.

The very effective design on the runner shown on page 40 is a good example of the modern application of Cross Stitch embroidery.

RUNNER

Materials required
Coats Anchor Stranded Cotton: 4 skeins Tapestry shade 0848; 3 skeins Cobalt Blue 0132; 2 skeins each Tapestry shade 0846, 0850 and Jade 0189. Use 4 strands throughout.

½ yd (45·7 cms) white evenweave embroidery fabric, 21 threads to 1 in. (2·5 cms), 36 in. (91·4 cms) wide.
1 Milward International Range tapestry needle No. 24.

The finished size of the runner is 33 ½ in. (85·1 cms) × 13 in. (33 cms).

Instructions
Mark the centre of fabric across both ways with a line of basting stitches. The Cross Stitch is worked over two threads of fabric, approximately 10 crosses to 1 in. (2·5 cms). The diagram gives a section of the repeating design, centres marked by blank arrows which should coincide with the basting stitches. Each background square of the diagram represents two threads of fabric. Follow the diagram and the sign key for the design and placing of colours.

Commence in the centre of fabric two threads from the crossed basting stitches and work the given section. Repeat from A to B twice more on the right-hand side and from C to D twice more on the left-hand side to complete.

Press the embroidery on the wrong side. Turn back 1 in. (2·5 cms) hem on all sides, mitre corners and slipstitch.

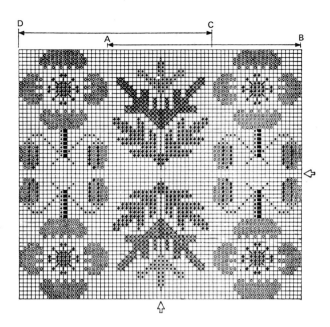

■ 0189
⊡ 0848
☒ 0850 Cross Stitch
⊡ 0846
⊞ 0132

⅃ 0189 Back Stitch

✦ 0132 Straight Stitch

These Cross Stitch flowers and leaf motifs and various combinations of them can be used to decorate a variety of articles. For example, two flower motifs with one leaf motif in the centre would look very attractive embroidered on the ends of a tray cloth or on a set of luncheon mats. A border of motifs worked across the centre of a cushion cover or two rows forming a decorative band on curtains, chair backs or a tablecloth would be striking and unusual.

It is not always realised that a design planned for Cross Stitch can be adapted quite easily for tapestry. (Full details for the working of tapestry are given on pages 68 and 69.) The most suitable yarn is Coats Anchor Tapisserie Wool which is made in a wide range of shades to conform with both modern and traditional colour schemes. Double thread canvas (10 holes to 1 in. [2.5 cms]) and single thread canvas (18 threads to 1 in. [2.5 cms]) are best for tapestry work. The stitches should be Gros Point on double thread canvas and Petit Point on single thread canvas, while Cross Stitch looks right on either. Depending upon the number of motifs used and their placing, designs for such articles as cushions, chair seats, stool tops and wall hangings can be developed from the chart shown at the top of this page.

Cut-work embroidery

Cut-work, in a variety of styles and patterns, has been popular in this country since the sixteenth century. At that time, it reached great perfection and many fine examples can be seen in contemporary portraits. The fashion spread from Italy and indeed many of the methods and stitches bear Italian names, such as Renaissance, Venetian and Reticella. The French developed their own style of Cut-work, which is widely known as Richelieu embroidery.

Designs   The designs used in Cut-work can be simple or elaborate, but in all cases the motifs, whether they be flowers, leaves or figures, are first outlined by rows of Buttonhole Stitch, sometimes joined by embroidered Buttonhole Stitch bars. Sections of the background fabric, between the motifs, are then cut out. Occasionally, surface stitchery is added to enhance the embroidery and give greater emphasis to selected shapes.

Contemporary   Today, contemporary Cut-work affords an interesting
Cut-work   alternative to free style embroidery. It is striking in appear-

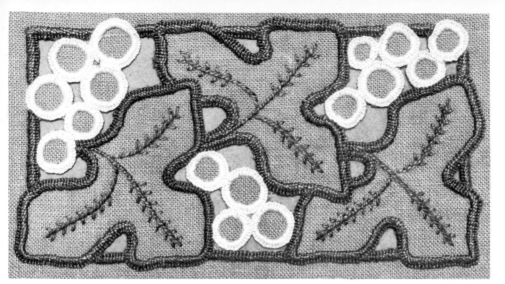

ance and though it has a lace-like quality, it is more durable than it appears. Cut-work is suitable for all household linen including table runners, teacloths, luncheon sets etc. If used on bedlinen, however, the designs selected should be simple and bold.

Fabrics and threads

Fabrics and threads should be chosen with care. In traditional pieces, white or natural linens were stitched with matching threads, but today the trend for colour in all furnishings means that there is no limit to the choice. It must be emphasised, however, that the selected fabric should be firmly woven, and slightly stiff, so that there is no fraying when the shapes or edges are cut. When coloured

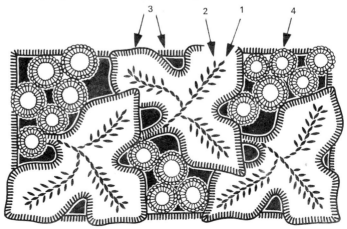

1. Stem stitch
2. Straight stitch
3. Buttonhole stitch
4. Buttonhole stitch

fabrics are used with contrasting threads, care must be taken to avoid harsh and clashing combinations of colour. Both Anchor Stranded Cotton and Pearl Cotton No. 8 may be used successfully – the former gives a smooth, shiny texture and the latter a rich purled finish.

Method of working The double lines of the design are filled in with closely worked Buttonhole Stitch, which must always be worked with the looped edge to the parts to be cut away. If Buttonhole Stitch bars appear in the design these should be worked first and care must be taken to keep the tension regular. When the embroidery is completed, press on the wrong side of the fabric. With very sharp pointed scissors, cut away the fabric along the edges from the wrong side, taking care not to snip the stitches. The parts marked × in the line drawing and the black areas in the diagram represent the areas in the article to be cut away. The leaf and berry design illustrated on page 42 can be used in a number of ways (see page 90 for suggestions for using embroidery motifs). Always place the design above the hem line unless the design is to form a continuous border.

ENLARGING A DESIGN

To enlarge a design, first trace it on to paper ruled into ½ in. (1·3 cms) squares. On a second piece of paper, the size which you want your finished design to appear, rule the same number of squares as are on the tracing. Now carefully copy the lines of the design, square by square, from the drawing to the second piece of paper, which can then be used as a pattern for your work.

The same method can, of course, be used to reduce the size of a design, the second piece of paper in this case being smaller than the original transfer.

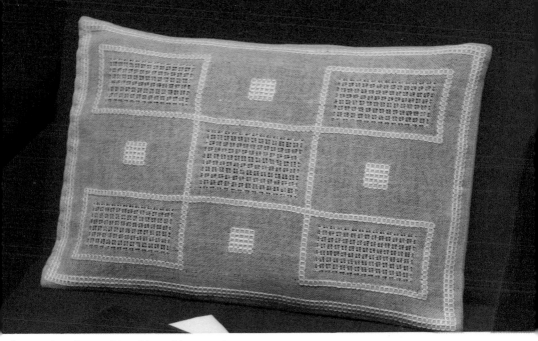

Instructions for working this cushion are given on pages 46–49

Drawn fabric embroidery

Drawn fabric embroidery is sometimes known as Pulled Thread Work. It is undoubtedly of peasant origin and is reputed to have originated in the Greek islands. From there, it spread to Italy, Germany, Belgium, Denmark and finally to England in the seventeenth and eighteenth centuries. In the textile departments of certain museums, examples of the work of that period can be seen and they are of a high standard and closely allied to needlepoint lace.

In earlier pieces the embroidery was worked on white or natural linens with matching threads, but with the contemporary vogue for colour, exciting effects are achieved by using coloured fabrics and threads to give a new look to this traditional embroidery. For greater richness of stitchery, surface stitches such as Satin Stitch and Back Stitch are often added.

Method of working

As can be appreciated from the name Drawn Fabric, the lacy designs are achieved by working certain stitches in such a way that the threads of the fabric are drawn or pulled

A close up of the lower left hand corner of the cushion cover

together in groups to form openwork patterns. All stitches are worked over a given number of threads of the fabric and the embroidery thread is always pulled firmly with each needle movement, so that spaces are formed between the fabric threads. Owing to the fact that no fabric threads are actually withdrawn the embroidery remains strong and durable and yet retains a certain fragile appearance.

Fabric selection

It is essential that the selected fabric be of evenweave i.e. with the same number of warp and weft threads to the square inch (cm) of fabric. The fabric must not be too closely woven so that the fabric threads can be drawn together with ease to produce 'holes' in the fabric texture. It must not be too fine to ensure easy counting of threads.

Choice of thread

The choice of thread is also important and to achieve the best lacy texture, should be slightly finer than the threads of the fabric. Anchor Stranded Cotton and Anchor Pearl Cotton No. 8 are suitable and give the desired effect.

CUSHION COVER

This simple geometric design has been built up by using blocks of Four-sided Stitch as shown in the detailed illustrations. The working diagram on page 48 shows part of the centre section of the design and the layout diagram gives one half of the design.

Materials required　Coats Anchor Stranded Cotton: 8 skeins white 0402. Use 3 strands for the five decorative oblong shapes; 6 strands for remainder of embroidery.

⅜ yd (34·3 cms) pale blue evenweave fabric, 21 threads to 1 in. (2·5 cms), 59 in. (149·7 cms) wide.

1 each Milward International Range tapestry needles Nos. 20 and 24 for 6 and 3 strands respectively.

The finished size of the cushion is approximately 12 in. × 18 in. (30·5 cms × 45·7 cms).

Method　Cut two pieces 13½ in. × 19½ in. (34·3 cms × 49·5 cms) from 59 in. (149·7 cms) wide. Mark the centre of one piece both ways with a line of basting stitches, these lines act as a guide when placing the design. The design is worked throughout in Four-Sided Stitch. The working diagram gives part of the centre section of the design, centre indicated by blank arrows which should coincide with the basting stitches. Diagram 1 also shows the arrangement of the stitches on the threads of the fabric represented by the background lines. The layout diagram gives the left-hand half of the design, centre indicated by blank arrows which should coincide with the basting stitches. The

A. This method of working Four-sided Stitch is the same as given on page 19, but at each stage the thread is pulled, thus producing a more lacy effect.

B. This time the alternate rows have been worked in Four-sided Stitch over two threads in groups of two, with one thread between each group.

C. This motif has been built up from diamonds and squares, formed by a Four-sided Stitch with Satin Stitch arrow-heads as the centre.

1. Working diagram

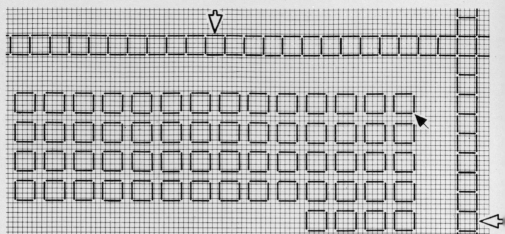

2. Layout
diagram

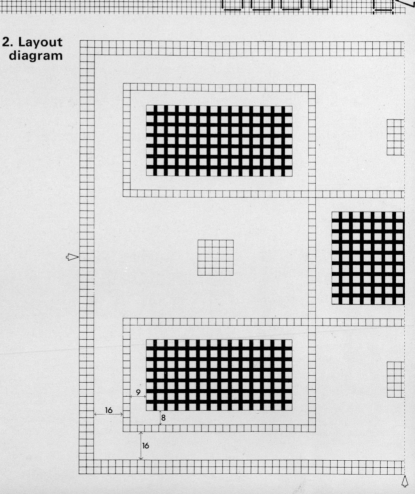

numerals indicate the number of threads between the rows of Four-Sided Stitch. The solid black lines indicate the two threads between each Four-Sided Stitch. With long side of fabric facing, commence the design at black arrow 22 threads up from the crossed basting stitches and 41 threads to the right, and work the section given, following the lay-out diagram for placing of design. The filling has 126 Four-Sided Stitches in all. These stitches which are worked in 3 strands are pulled firmly. Work the other half to correspond. Press embroidery on wrong side. Trim margins even, allowing ½ in. (1·3 cms) for seams and leaving ¼ in. (6 mms) from embroidery.

woman's jacket embroidered in black silk on linen, in speckling, stem, braid and back stitch. Early 17th century

Hardanger Luncheon Set

Hardanger embroidery

Hardanger, a mountainous region in Norway, is famed all over the world for its traditional openwork embroidery. The designs in this type of embroidery are built up from regular groups of Satin Stitches known as 'Kloster' blocks, each block comprised of an uneven number of stitches. Certain of these blocks are worked so that they outline small squares of fabric and when the embroidery is completed, the fabric threads of some of these squares are cut away and withdrawn as required. The loose threads are overcast or woven to form bars, and various filling stitches are worked within the spaces left by the drawn threads. Due to the stitch formation, Hardanger designs are geometrical in form, making square, oblong, triangular or diamond shapes.

Traditional Hardanger pieces – many fine examples can be found in the museums of Oslo and Bergen – were worked on fine white linen with matching thread. However, in the modern interpretations of Hardanger embroidery a heavier fabric (for ease of counting) and brightly coloured embroidery thread have been used.

Fabric The selected fabric must be of evenweave i.e. having the same number of warp and weft threads to the square inch (cm). Also it must not be too fine to ensure easy counting of threads and stitches – fabric with 29 threads to 1 IN. (2·5 cms) is recommended.

Threads The threads ideally suitable for Hardanger Embroidery are Anchor Pearl Cotton Nos. 5 and 8; No. 5 is used for the bold 'Kloster' blocks and No. 8 for the bars and delicate fillings which occur in certain of the spaces.

Standard working procedure There is a sequence for the working of Hardanger Embroidery and this should always be followed so that no thread cutting mistakes occur.

1. Work all kloster blocks.
2. Work all additional surface stitches – lines, borders etc.
3. Cut and withdraw the threads for the open spaces.
4. Complete all the bars of the larger open spaces.
5. Add all decorative fillings, wheels etc.

HARDANGER LUNCHEON SET

Instructions for working the Hardanger luncheon set, together with a working diagram, are given overleaf.

A view of the mat

52

Materials required Coats Anchor Pearl Cotton No. 5 (10 grm. ball); 2 balls Rose Pink 054.
Coats Anchor Pearl Cotton No. 8 (10 grm. ball); 1 ball Rose Pink 054. Use Pearl Cotton No. 8 for Overcast Bars and fillings, No. 5 for remainder of embroidery.

½ yd (45·7 cms) white, fine evenweave fabric, 29 threads to 1 in. (2·5 cms), 52 in. (131·8 cms) wide.
1 each Milward International Range tapestry needles Nos. 20 and 24 for Pearl Cotton Nos. 5 and 8 respectively.

The finished size of centre mat is 16 in. (40·6 cms) square, place mats 12 in. × 16 in. (30·5 cms × 40·6 cms).

Suitable fabric brand is Glenshee evenweave linen (ivory).

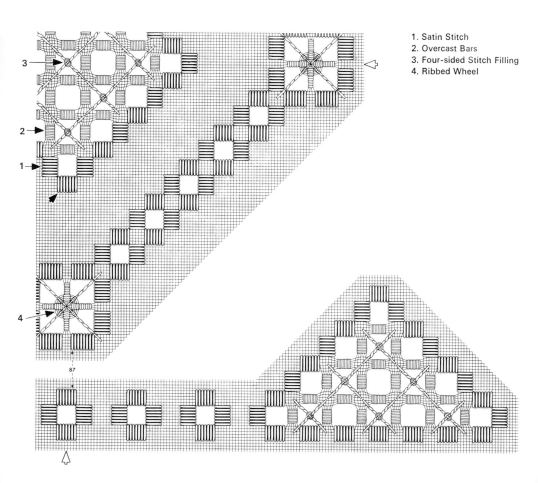

1. Satin Stitch
2. Overcast Bars
3. Four-sided Stitch Filling
4. Ribbed Wheel

Method Cut one piece from fabric 17½ in. (44·5 cms) square for centre mat and two pieces of 13½ in. × 17½ in. (34·3 cms × 44·5 cms) for place mats. Mark the centre both ways on each piece with a line of basting stitches. The diagram gives a little more than one quarter of the design used on the square mat. The centre is indicated by blank arrows which should coincide with the basting stitches. The diagram also shows the arrangement of the stitches on the threads of the fabric, represented by the background lines. The blank areas show where the threads have been cut out and the small numbers indicate the number of threads between the centre section of the design and the border.

Commence the embroidery at black arrow, 45 threads down from the crossed basting stitches and three threads to the left. Work one quarter as given following the diagram and number key for the embroidery. Work the other three quarters to correspond.

On place mats, with narrow end facing, work border section only, commencing at lower blank arrow 1 in. (2·5 cms) from edge. Work in reverse from blank arrow on to left-hand side. Turn fabric and repeat on opposite end. The Satin Stitch blocks should all be worked before the fabric is cut neatly from the sections which are enclosed by Satin Stitch blocks, and shown blank on the diagram. For sections where the centres are filled, cut and withdraw 6 threads, miss 6, cut 6 as required. Overcast the remaining loose threads and work the fillings. Press the embroidery on the wrong side. Make up, taking ½ in. (1·3 cms) hems on all sides, mitre corners and slipstitch.

Jacobean embroidery

It is the style of design, rather than the stitchery that is the Jacobean characteristic feature of embroidery. The designs were developed from oriental embroideries and fabrics which were brought to Britain during the Jacobean period. The glorious colours, the rich patterns, and the decorative leaf and flower shapes were accepted with delight by English embroiderers.

JACOBEAN MOTIF

Although inspired by traditional patterns, this design has been given a modern slant. Alterations to the accepted Jacobean style have been subtly made and the diverse colouring of the original pattern is replaced by bold but simple colours. At the same time, the complicated stitchery of the period has been translated into effective, but less

intricate, stitch arrangements. This attractive motif may be used on a variety of articles.

Traycloth　The traycloth shown opposite effectively uses the Jacobean motif, which is placed in opposite corners. The line drawing on the next page gives the outlines and some of the filling details. The working diagram and key on this page provide a complete guide to the actual stitches used.

Jacobean embroidery may be worked on any firmly woven fabric, linen, cotton or wool. The choice of embroidery thread is wide. Anchor Stranded Cotton, Soft Embroidery, Pearl Cotton No. 8 or Tapisserie Wool may be used depending upon the weight of the fabric and the effect desired.

Working diagram

1 – 0329	
2 – 0334	Stem Stitch
3 – 0905	
4 – 0381	
5 – 0334	Satin Stitch
6 – 0903	
7 – 0334	Blanket Stitch
8 – 0381	
9 – 0334	
10 – 0905	Chain Stitch
11 – 0381	
12 – 0329	Herringbone Stitch
13 – 0381	Twisted Chain Stitch
14 – 0903	Fly Stitch
15 – 0903	French Knots

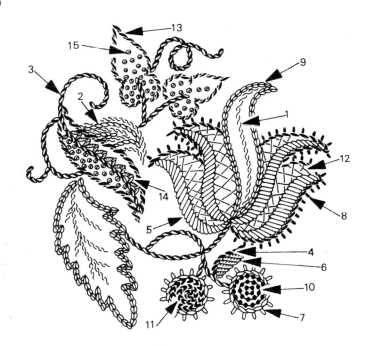

Norweave embroidery

Norweave or Åkle embroidery is extremely popular in Norway today. The original concept was inspired by traditional bedcovers woven in brightly coloured geometric patterns. All the designs are built up from 'blocks' of stitches, which can vary in number, the length depending upon whether a double or single thread canvas is used.

It is interesting to note that over the years the simple primary colours used originally have given way to vivid modern colours and that the designs have progressed from geometric, mosaic style patterns to a graphic style of design using flowers, birds and outdoor scenes as a new source of inspiration.

WALL HANGING

This type of embroidery has a wide variety of uses. The attractive wall hanging illustrated overleaf shows a quick and easy way of using this colourful new style of embroidery. Working diagram is given on page 59.

Materials required Coats Anchor Tapisserie Wool: 7 skeins 0160; 6 skeins 0902; 4 skeins each 0185, 0400; 3 skeins each 0162, 0390; 2 skeins each 0217, 0279, 0311, 0332, 0375, 0398, 0402, 0412, 0849, 0850, 0859, 0860; 1 skein each 0118, 0203, 0239, 0336, 0391 and 0869.
1 yd (91·4 cms) double thread tapestry canvas, 27 in. (68·2 cms) wide, 10 holes to 1 in. (2·5 cms).
¾ yd (68·2 cms) grey medium weight fabric, 36 in. (91·4 cms) wide, for backing.
1 wooden rod or cane, approximately 24 in. (60·7 cms) long × ⅝ in. (1·6 cms) diameter.
1 yd (91·4 cms) matching cord, approximately ⅜ in. (1 cm) thick.
1 Milward International Range tapestry needle No. 18.
The finished size of the illustrated wall hanging is approximately 31 in. × 21 in. (78·9 cms × 53 cms).

Suitable canvas brand is: Penelope double thread tapestry canvas, ecru, K119.

Working diagram

−0118
−0160
−0162
−0185
−0203
−0217
−0239
−0279
−0311
−0332
−0336
−0375
−0390
−0391
−0398
−0400
−0402
−0412
−0849
−0850
−0859
−0860
−0869
−0902
− 0375 Couching

Instructions   Mark the centre of canvas both ways with a line of basting stitches running along a line of holes widthwise, and between a pair of narrow double threads lengthwise. Page 59 shows the complete design with the centre marked by black arrows which should coincide with the basting stitches. Each background square of the diagram represents one block of three double Satin Stitches over three double threads of canvas. Commence the embroidery centrally, following page 59 and the sign key. The masts are worked last; the couched threads are double thickness caught down by a tying stitch of single thickness in the same shade, between every horizontal row of double Satin Stitch.

To make up   Trim canvas to within 2 in. (5 cms) of embroidery at upper edge and 1 in. (2·5 cms) at sides and lower edge. Cut a piece from backing fabric the same size as canvas. Place both pieces right sides together and sew lower edge and two sides close to the embroidery, to within 4 in. (10·2 cms) of upper raw edge. To make a channel for the rod turn in 1 in. (2·5 cms) unworked canvas at the sides of upper edge, then fold over the 2 in. (5 cms) margin of unworked canvas level with finished edge of embroidery, and lightly catch-stitch the raw edge to wrong side. Turn to right side; turn in backing fabric seam allowance at top edge and sides and slipstitch together. Insert rod. Attach cord at each end of the rod.

Shadow work embroidery

Shadow work is one of the most delicate and beautiful types of embroidery, and fits in happily in the modern home. It is thought to be of Indian origin and until recently was mainly worked with white thread on white fabric.

The use of transparent fabrics and a 'shadowy' effect on the right side of the fabric are typical of this form of embroidery. The shadow effect is created by Closed Herringbone Stitch embroidery on the reverse side of the fabric, and can be highlighted further by other embroidery stitches worked on the right side.

The leaf and berry design illustrated overleaf

Fabric Originally organdie was the favourite fabric, but today the selection of suitable transparent fabrics is much wider and colour in both thread and fabric can now be introduced in this embroidery. Bright colours used on the back of pale transparent fabrics create an almost opalescent effect on the front, whereas the traditional white on white gives a more cool and sophisticated finish.

SHADOW WORK MOTIF

The leaf and berry motif illustrated can be applied to a variety of articles. The diagram gives stitch details. See page 90 for some suggestions for using this motif.

Working diagram

1 – 0216 | Shadow Work
2 – 086 |
3 – 086 | Satin Stitch
4 – 0216 | Back Stitch

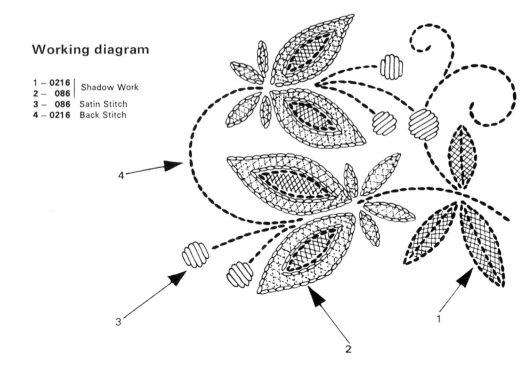

Smocking

Smocking is a decorative method of gathering a width of fabric into regular folds.

It is of peasant origin and the word 'smock' comes from the Anglo-Saxon word for a shirt. Farm workers throughout the centuries wore a loose tunic or shirt, shaped at the yoke by means of bands of stitchery which pulled the fabric together into regular folds. As the years went on, the patterns of stitchery became more elaborate and designs were developed which indicated the occupation of the wearer. Examples were crooks and hearts for shepherds, trees and leaves for woodmen, and wheels for a carter.

Today the practical purpose of smocking is the decorative control of fullness on a garment, at yoke, waist or cuff. It is ideal for use on babies' and children's clothes, where elasticity and freedom for expansion and growth are an important factor.

BASIC SMOCKING

Fabric A wide range of fabrics can be used, the choice depending upon the style and purpose of the garment. The selected fabric can be of fine to medium weight but it must not be heavy or rigid as then the folds would hang too stiffly. Any plain, fine fabric such as cotton, silk, organdie, terylene lawn etc. can be used or a fabric with a ¼ in. (6 mms) woven check such as voile or gingham.

Other materials Anchor Stranded Cotton (3 strands) or Anchor Pearl Cotton No. 8 for smocking.
Coats Drima (polyester) thread for gathering.
Milward International Range crewel needle No. 6.

Transfer instructions When smocking is to be worked on a plain fabric, a transfer, consisting of rows of equally spaced dots, is used. The transfer requires to be at least three times the length of the finished measurement e.g. if an 8 in. (20·3 cms) section of smocking is required, at least 24 in. (60·7 cms) will be needed.

   Pin the transfer securely face downwards on to the fabric. Apply a fairly hot iron with pressure, taking care not to crease or move the paper in any way. For a fine transparent fabric the transfer should be basted in position on the wrong side of the fabric. The rows of dots are picked up through the paper and fabric then the paper is removed. When a slightly less transparent fabric is used, iron the required amount of transfer on to the wrong side of the fabric.

   On a fabric with a ¼ in. (6 mms) woven check, no transfer is required. The rows of gathering are worked by picking up a small stitch in the centre of all crossed lines of fabric.

Instructions for gathering Commence the gathering on the wrong side of fabric using a separate thread for each row. Start at the right-hand side with a knot and a small back stitch to secure the thread and pick up a small portion of the fabric on each dot (see diagram). Leave a loose thread at end of each row. Draw up the rows of stitching to form gathers but do not pull too tightly as the gathers must be flexible in order to work the

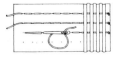

smocking. Tie the loose ends firmly in pairs close to the last fold. When working the smocking stitches do not pull too tightly as the finished work must have elasticity.

The accompanying diagram shows the stitch scheme for the sampler illustrated on page 63. The stitch numbering corresponds with the numbered stitch diagrams given below.

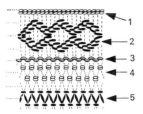

Once the gathering has been completed, follow the appropriate stitch diagrams. When the smocking has been completed, place a damp cloth over the wrong side of smocking and pass a hot iron lightly over until work is completely dry. Do not use pressure. Remove the gathering threads.

Outline stitch

DIAGRAM 1. Secure the thread and bring the needle through on the first pleat. Pick up the top of the next pleat inserting the needle with a slight slope and leaving the thread above the needle. This stitch is worked with the thread over two pleats, but only one pleat is picked up by each stitch.

Feather stitch

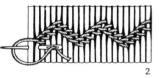

DIAGRAM 2. Secure thread on first pleat at right-hand side. Take first and second pleats together with thread held under the needle point and slightly below; take second and third pleats together, and in the same manner third and fourth, fourth and fifth, fifth and sixth pleats (this completes the downward slope). Work four stitches in upward slope to correspond, taking sixth and seventh pleats together, seventh and eighth, eighth and ninth, ninth and tenth pleats. The diagram shows position of thread for downward slope; for upward slope the thread is held to the other side of the needle but still passes under the needle point.

Cable stitch

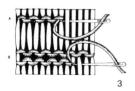

DIAGRAM 3. Secure thread on first pleat on left-hand side. This stitch is worked over two pleats by taking up one pleat with the needle, the thread being alternately above and below the needle. Section A – one row of cable stitch with the needle movement showing thread below the needle; Section B – two rows worked closely together with the second needle movement showing thread above the needle.

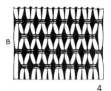

Honeycomb stitch

DIAGRAM 4. Secure the thread on first pleat on left-hand side, then take first and second pleats together with two small satin stitches. In the last stitch pass the needle down through the second pleat and work two stitches over second and third pleats. Pass needle through third pleat and take two Satin Stitches over third and fourth pleats. Figure A shows the needle movement. Continue in this manner until desired number of rows are completed. Figure B shows two rows of Honeycomb stitch.

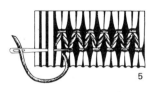

Surface honeycomb stitch

DIAGRAM 5. Secure the thread at the left-hand side and bring the needle through on first pleat on top level. Draw the needle horizontally through the second pleat with the thread above the needle, with thread still above, insert the needle horizontally through the same pleat on lower level. With the thread below the needle, insert the needle horizontally through the third pleat on lower level and still with the thread below, insert the needle through the same pleat on top level. Continue in this way to end of row.

Detail of a bed-curtain embroidered by Abigail Pett in the 17th century. It is worked in long and short stitch, split, stem and feather stitches

Part of a sampler embroidered in England during the reign of
Charles I. It is worked chiefly in tent stitch on linen with silk and
gold thread. The actual sampler is 11½ inches (29·3 cms) wide.

Tapestry

Tapestry, or to give it the correct name, needlework Tapestry, is the art of embroidering with the needle and thread upon canvas in such a way that the canvas is completely covered and the effect of woven fabric is obtained. A wide variety of stitches can be used on canvas, but when producing tapestry the principal stitch used is Tent Stitch. Tent Stitch is the general name which covers both Gros Point Stitch and Petit Point Stitch. The difference is that the first is worked over double thread canvas and the second over fine single thread canvas. This, of course, makes the latter stitch smaller than the former. These stitches, owing to their construction, have a diagonal pull, so all tapestry work should be mounted and worked on a square or oblong frame.

This embroidery technique is most suitable for cushions, chair seats, stool tops, wall hangings and panels.

A tapestry frame with adjustable sides

Important rules There are certain important rules which *must* be observed when working tapestry

1. Buy all yarn at the same time, particularly that for the background. Dyes vary and you may not be able to match the colours exactly if you run short.

2. Use a square or oblong frame, wide enough for the whole area of the canvas to be stretched. On large pieces the end of the canvas may have to be rolled. A circular ring or round frame is not suitable.

3. Leave at least 3 in. (7·5 cms) of unworked canvas all round in order to make the stretching and mounting easier.

4. Use Gros Point Stitch with a Trammed Stitch on double thread canvas to ensure that the threads of the canvas are completely covered.

5. Make every stitch of Gros Point or Petit Point in two movements.

6. Work to an even tension, allowing the wool to fill each hole.

7. Do not begin or end the work with knots, as they stand out in relief when the work is finally stretched and mounted. To start, push the needle through the canvas on the right side about 2 in. (5 cms) from the point of working, leaving a short end. When the section of the tapestry is complete, darn in the end on the wrong side and trim away the surplus.

8. Work the background area in staggered lengths, not squared blocks, so that the surface texture is smooth and no ridges are formed. Use varying lengths of thread.

9. Use a shorter length of embroidery thread than normal, as the action of being pulled through the canvas tends to fray the thread.

TAPESTRY PICTURES *Illustrated on pages 70 and 71*

Materials required

FOR PICTURE A – Coats Anchor Tapisserie Wool: 4 skeins 0403; 1 skein each 095, 096, 097, 099, 0215, 0216, 0217, 0265, 0298 and 0305.

FOR PICTURE B – Coats Anchor Tapisserie Wool: 4 skeins 0403; 1 skein each 0213, 0265, 0266, 0268, 0288, 0314, 0340 and 0402.

¼ yd (23 cms) double thread tapestry canvas, 19 in. (48·2 cms) wide, 10 holes to 1 in. (2·5 cms).

2 picture frames with mounting board or cardboard 5 in. × 7 in. (12·7 cms × 17·8 cms).

1 Milward International Range tapestry needle No. 18.

PICTURE A : ANEMONE

A working diagram is given on page 72

PICTURE B : CHRISTMAS ROSES

A working diagram is given on page 73

Working diagram A

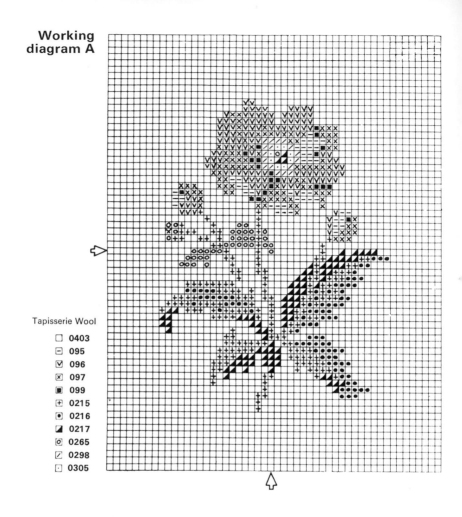

Tapisserie Wool

- ☐ 0403
- ⊟ 095
- ☑ 096
- ☒ 097
- ▣ 099
- ⊞ 0215
- ⊙ 0216
- ◩ 0217
- ⊡ 0265
- ⊘ 0298
- ⊡ 0305

Working instructions

Cut two pieces from canvas 7 in. × 9 in. (17·8 cms × 23 cms). The larger measurement should be along the selvedge. Mount on tapestry frame: see page 13. Mark across centre both ways with a line of basting stitches. Diagrams A and B give the complete designs, centres marked by blank arrows which coincide with the basting stitches. Each background square of the diagrams represents the double thread of canvas. The design is worked throughout in Trammed Gros Point Stitch. Commence embroidery centrally at crossed basting stitches and follow the diagram and sign key.

**Working
diagram B**

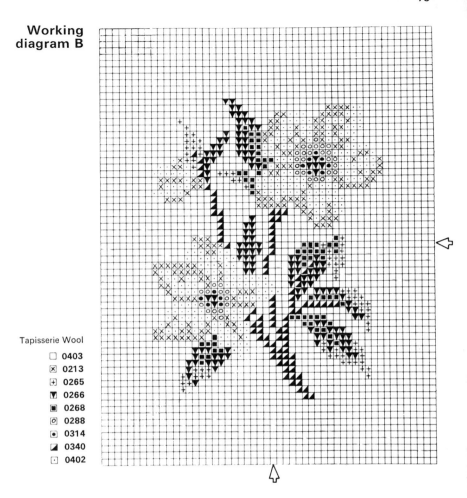

Tapisserie Wool

- ☐ 0403
- ⊠ 0213
- ⊞ 0265
- ▼ 0266
- ▣ 0268
- ◯ 0288
- ● 0314
- ◢ 0340
- ⊡ 0402

Making up If the embroidered piece of canvas is pulled very much out
of shape it may be dampened then pinned and stretched to
the correct shape on a clean dry board, using rustless drawing pins. Leave to dry for 2 to 3 weeks. Canvas work need
not be pressed. When the stretched canvas is dry, place
it on heavy cardboard, fold the surplus edges to the back
and secure at top with pins into edge of cardboard. Secure
at the back by lacing both ways with a strong thread.
Remove pins and place in frame.

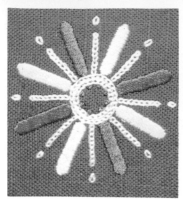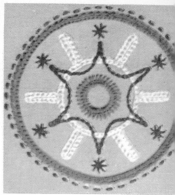

Embroidery designing

Inspiration for design in embroidery can be found in a wide variety of subjects. These range through natural forms to geometric and abstract shapes. The ancient Greeks, who were the masters of geometry, evolved countless repeating geometric patterns to enrich their pottery and architecture.

Colour also plays an important feature in all embroidery and the use of brilliant fabrics and harmonious colour schemes opens up exciting possibilities to the designer.

DESIGNING WITH CIRCULAR SHAPES

By developing and elaborating varying sizes of circles a number of motifs suitable for interpretation in embroidery can be designed. As a preliminary, the circles can be divided into six, eight or ten equal parts to form a basic structure upon which are built patterns of concentric circles, zig-zag lines, straight lines, curved lines, spots and stars. Variety and interest can be added by the choice of stitchery and texture can be introduced by the contrast of smooth or broken lines with solid areas. A further note of interest is achieved by varying the thickness of thread used.

Suggestions for arrangement and stitches When an embroidered motif has been developed from a circle some thought must be given to the placing of this motif to form a harmonious design, perhaps by repeating it to form a border or setting out a regular formation to provide an all-over pattern. Remember when planning the

design that the size of the circle and the number of circles must be in proportion to the size of the article and the area to be decorated. A small, delicate ring or spot would be suitable for fine embroidery worked on a blouse or lingerie, while a cushion or curtain in heavier fabric would require a bold motif larger in size and heavier in texture.

Circular motifs can be adapted to decorate a wide variety of articles.

WORKBAG *Shown above*
Materials required

Coats Anchor Stranded Cotton: 3 skeins Peacock Blue 0170; 2 skeins each Flame 0333 and White 0402. Use 6 strands for blue Back Stitch, 2 strands for white Back Stitch and white Stem Stitch, 3 strands for rest of embroidery.

½ yd (45·7 cms) fine green embroidery fabric, 36 in. (91·4 cms) wide, ½ yd (45·7 cms) fine blue fabric for lining.

Instructions for working this circular motif are given on p. 77

1 each Milwards International Range crewel needles Nos. 5 and 6 (6 strands, 2 and 3 respectively).

7 in. (17.8 cms) square of Vilene, or other bonded fibre fabric.

2 yd (1m 83 cms) Blue twisted cord.

1 reel each Coats Drima (polyester) thread to match green and blue fabric.

Finished size of bag 17 in. (43.2 cms) deep × 28½ in. (72.3 cms) circumference.

Instructions Cut 29½ in × 18 in. (74.8 cms × 45.7 cms) from green and blue fabric. Cut 6½ in. (16.5 cms) circle from green and blue fabric and from Vilene for base. ½ in. (1.3 cms) is allowed on all pieces for seams. Fold back ½ in. (1.3 cms) on each narrow end of green fabric and press. Copy the motifs shown below, enlarging them if you wish, and trace down, repeating 6 times across fabric 3½ in. (8.8 cms) from the lower edge, commencing and finishing with half the small motifs at the folded ends. This ensures continuity of the design when side seam is joined. Follow the stitch diagram opposite and the number key for the embroidery. All parts similar to numbered parts are worked in same colour and stitch. Press the embroidery on the wrong side.

See page 44 for a note on enlarging designs.

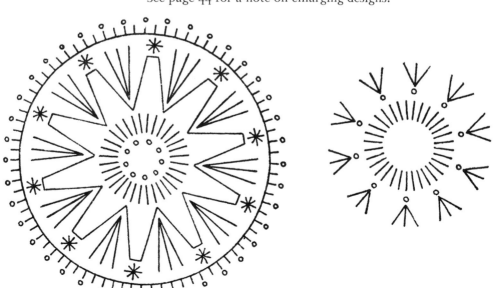

To make up Join narrow ends of embroidered fabric to make a cylinder. Baste together circles of green and blue fabric with Vilene sandwiched between. Mark the green base into 8 equal sections with pins. Mark the lower edge of embroidered fabric into 8 equal parts with pins. Align the pins on green base and embroidered fabric, right sides together and make tucks from surplus fabric to fit base. Stitch together $\frac{1}{2}$ in. (1·3 cms) from the edges. Press seams and turn to right side. With side seam to back of bag, make a buttonhole $\frac{1}{2}$ in. (1·3 cms) deep on each side 3 in. (7·5 cms) from top edge. Join narrow ends of lining and press seam. Place lining over bag right sides together, top edges even and stitch round $\frac{1}{2}$ in. (1·3 cms) from top edge. Turn lining to right side. Press top edge. Mark and tuck the raw edge in same way as for bag. Turn in $\frac{1}{2}$ in. (1·3 cms) at lower edge, place lining inside bag and slipstitch the lower edge to base, covering the base seam. Work 2 rows of machine stitching $\frac{1}{2}$ in. (1·3 cms) apart round bag, with the buttonholes between the rows to make cord channel. Cut twisted cord in half. Thread one cord round the channel bringing it out again through the same buttonhole. Join the ends and neaten with a blue tassel. Thread the second cord through the other buttonhole and finish in same way to make drawstrings. Remove basting stitches.

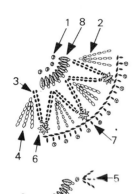

1 – **0402** – French Knots
2 – **0402**
3 – **0170** Back Stitch
4 – **0402**
5 – **0170** Stem Stitch
6 – **0333** – Double Cross Stitch
7 – **0170** – Blanket Stitch
8 – **0333** – Daisy Stitch

CIRCULAR MOTIF (See page 75)

The accompanying stitch diagram and key give working details for this attractive motif.

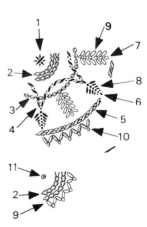

1 – **0169** – Double Cross Stitch
2 – **0333** – Chain Stitch
3 – **0402** – Back Stitch
4 – **0169**
5 – **0333** Twisted Chain Stitch
6 – **0169**
7 – **0402** Straight Stitch
8 – **0169**
9 – **0402** Fly Stitch
10 – **0333**
11 – **0402** – French Knots

DESIGNING WITH BIRD SHAPES

Birds are an everyday sight and provide an easy basic shape for study and elaboration.

If you look closely at different birds, exotic ones with gloriously coloured plumage or ordinary drab or speckled ones, you will realise that, although the birds themselves are of many sizes, all the body shapes are in fact a simple egg-shape, oval with one end more pointed than the other. On further study you will see that every bird differs in the shapes to be seen in beaks, wings, legs, tail feathers, or crests.

Find the correct angle

Experiment with the angle at which the body shape is placed so that the birds are standing sideways or, seen from the back, looking over one shoulder. The angle of the body contributes to the liveliness of the design.

Deciding on suitable stitch

Having decided upon the design of the bird, thought can be given to the embroidery, which must be both decorative and suitable for the selected fabric and finished article. A number of basic embroidery stitches such as Detached Chain Stitch, Fly Stitch, French Knots, Buttonhole and Herringbone Stitch, can be used in combination or one stitch may be used on each bird (not including outlining). This may sound monotonous but if you try embroidering one stitch in a variety of sizes, putting large stitches next to small ones and varying the thickness of the thread, you will be surprised by the interesting finished effect. Do not work regularly in rows but scatter the stitches, packing some tightly together and placing others further apart. This will make unusual textures. Experiment with just one stitch and see what you can do to achieve individual results. Alternatively a selection of well-chosen stitches can produce an exciting variety of line and texture.

BAG (*Shown opposite*)

Materials required

Coats Anchor Stranded Cotton: 1 skein each Cyclamen 088, Jade 0188, Amber Gold 0309, Tangerine 0313, Coffee 0380 and White 0402. Use 6 strands for Double Knot Stitch, White Chain Stitch, White Back Stitch and Coffee Daisy Stitch; use 4 strands for White Stem Stitch and Brown

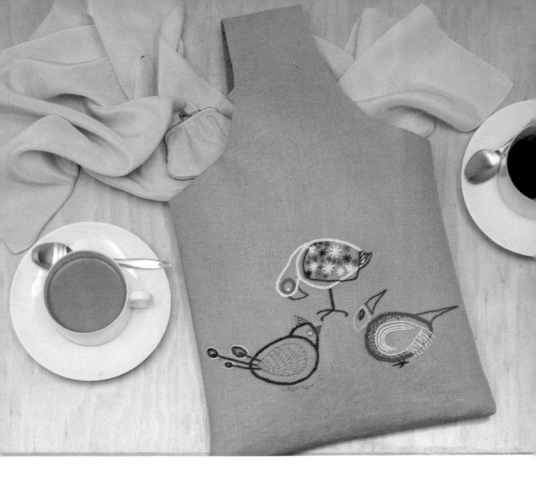

Chain Stitch; the Straight Stitch Stars vary from 6 strands to 1 strand according to size; the Buttonhole Stitch varies from 6 strands to 1 strand working from right to left; use 3 strands for rest of embroidery.

⅜ yd (34·3 cms) medium weight lime green fabric, as in illustration, 48 in. (121·9 cms) wide.

⅜ yd (34·3 cms) fine fabric in desired colour, 36 in. (91·4 cms) wide, for lining.

1 piece 11 in. × 36 in. (28 cms × 91·4 cms) Vilene, or other bonded fibre interlining.

1 reel Coats Drima (polyester) thread to match linen.

1 each Milward International Range crewel needles Nos. 5, 6 and 8 (for 6 strands, 4 and 3 strands, 2 and 1 strand respectively). The finished size of the bag is 17½ in. × 11 in. (44·5 cms × 28 cms).

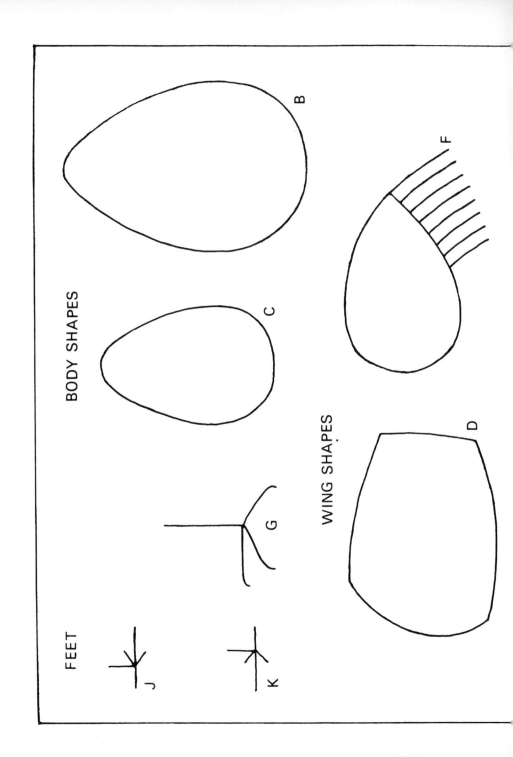

BODY SHAPES

B

C

FEET

J

K

WING SHAPES

D

F

G

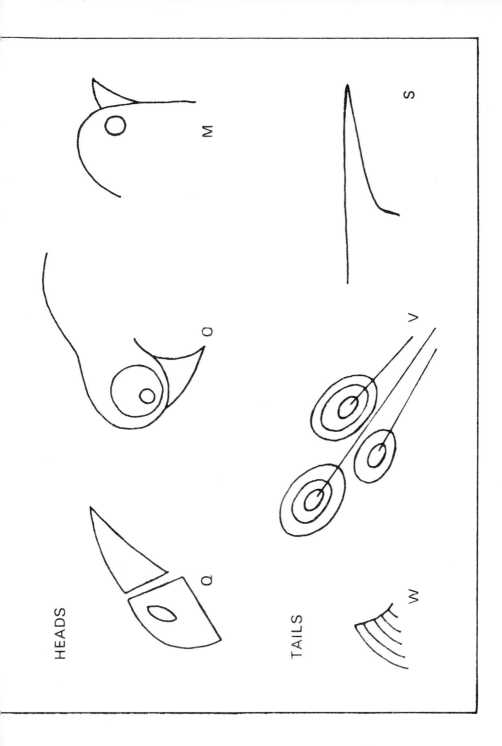

HEADS

M

O

Q

TAILS

S

V

W

Instructions The layout diagram gives half of the bag shape; 1 square equals 1 in. (2·5 cms). With dotted line to fold, cut one piece each by pattern from green fabric, lining and interlining.

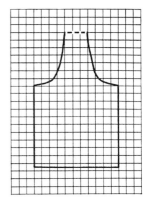

The design can be constructed by using the shapes shown on pages 80, 81, B, D, G, O and W for upper bird; B, C, J, M, V and W for left-hand bird and B, F, Q and S for right-hand bird. Trace design on to fabric (see page 14 for tracing instructions).

Follow working diagram and number key for details of embroidery. All parts similar to numbered parts are worked in same colour stitch. Press the embroidery on the wrong side.

Making up With right sides of main piece together, machine stitch sides and lower edge ½ in. (1·3 cms) from edge. Press seams and turn to right side. Make up interlining in same way, trim seams and place in bag. Trim seam allowance from interlining on upper edges, turn fabric over interlining and herringbone stitch in position. Make up lining in same way; insert in bag; turn in seam allowance on upper edges and slipstitch to bag.

1 – 088		
2 – 0188		
3 – 0313	Stem Stitch	
4 – 0380		
5 – 0402		
6 – 088		
7 – 0313	Satin Stitch	
8 – 0402		
9 – 0188		
10 – 0313	Back Stitch	
11 – 0380		
12 – 0402		
13 – 0309		
14 – 0380	Chain Stitch	
15 – 0402		
16 – 088		
17 – 0309	Straight Stitch	
18 – 0380	Stars	
19 – 0402		
20 – 0188	Straight Stitch	
21 – 0380		
22 – 088	Daisy Stitch	
23 – 0380		
24 – 088	Double Knot Stitch	
25 – 088	Seeding	
26 – 0188	Buttonhole Stitch	

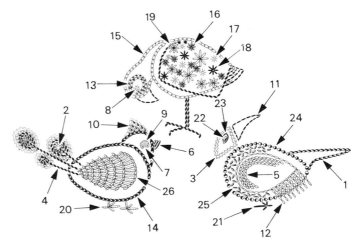

DESIGNING WITH A FLORAL SPRAY

Flowers and leaves have inspired countless embroidery designers in countries throughout the world. Even in Africa, where the craft of embroidery has been practised by very few of the tribes, primitive designs built round flowers have been found in Uganda.

From the sometimes over-decorative patterns of Jacobean embroidery to the starkly simple fruit and leaves of contemporary Scandinavia, the beauty of plant form has been an inspiration for centuries. Sources of design abound in flowers, leaves and berries of every variety.

From a passing glance at plants and flowers in a garden, we are only aware of an impression of colour, but a closer look reveals a wealth of detail and intricacy of shape and line. It is for us to select, and subsequently simplify, that part of the plant which suits our design requirements. Upon the word simplify rests the success of our venture into designing with flowers. This simplification of shape cannot be too strongly emphasised. If we attempt to include every detail of the chosen flower or leaf, we shall almost certainly end with confusion of design and pattern.

Having established that simplicity is vital to the standard of our design, we must now decide which part of the plant we shall use for embroidery – a flower head, fully opened or half-closed; a bud; a turning leaf; a tracery of veins or

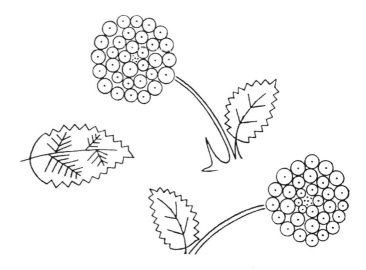

Stages in the development of a design

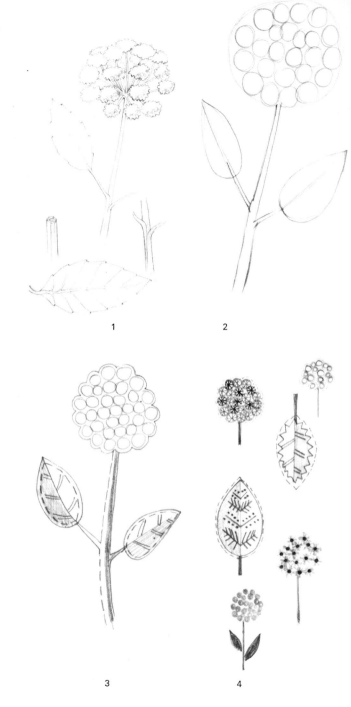

1

2

3

4

bold flower and leaf shapes springing from an elaborately patterned stalk – all these and many more provide inspiration for our designs.

Development of a design

On the facing page are shown four stages in the development of a design based on flowers and leaves.

1. One of several sketchbook studies, examining in some detail the form and structure of the chosen plant.
2. The first attempt at simplification, picking out the principal characteristics of the particular flower.
3. A further stage, showing a more marked adaptation suitable to the technique of embroidery.
4. The final stylised leaf and flower shapes.

Although completely stylised designs, the essential individualities of form and structure are retained, as in the original drawing.

A stitch sampler
(*see next page*)

Stitches Try a stitch sampler, similar to the one illustrated on page 85, and find for yourself the variations possible with one simple design and alternative stitch treatments, the different stitches giving different effects. Try adding a heavy line for emphasis or a broken line for lightness, always aiming to retain the main characteristics of the chosen plant.

Arrangement Finally, comes the arrangement of motifs on the article to be embroidered. There are many design possibilities in plant motifs and by experimentation and repetition, exciting designs can be developed for small borders as well as large central motifs.

DESIGN ADAPTATION

In free-style embroidery a design may be altered by the choice of thread and fabric. The following points should be noted:

1. The contrast of shiny and matt finish of threads, Stranded Cotton with Soft Embroidery or Tapisserie Wool with Stranded Cotton, or Pearl Cotton with Tapisserie Wool.

2. The contrast of thin thread and thick thread.

3. A design worked over a coarse fabric may be larger in scale than if it is worked over a fine fabric.

4. When the texture of the fabric is altered, it may be preferable to work a row of small stitches in place of one Straight Stitch.

DESIGNING WITH TEAR-DROP SHAPES

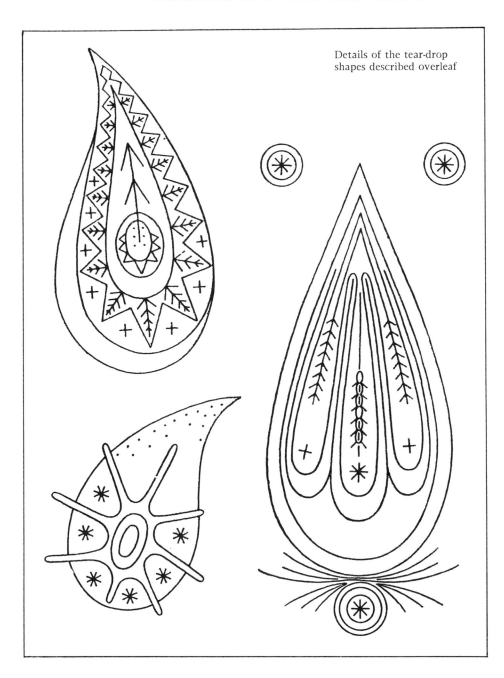

Details of the tear-drop
shapes described overleaf

Planning designs for embroidery need not be an elaborate or laborious process. Some of the most effective results can be obtained by using a very simple shape as a foundation for a design.

One such simple shape – the tear-drop shape – can be used as a basis for many varieties of pattern arrangement. This basic tear-drop shape remains the same in the example of embroidery shown above, although it varies slightly in size and outline.

Stitches   When carrying out the actual embroidery the stitch used for outlining the tear-drop shape may be varied to suit individual requirements. The inner area of this basic shape may also be divided up in different ways by a variety of embroidery stitches. To give interesting textures and outlines, the number of strands of thread may also be varied.

Working diagram

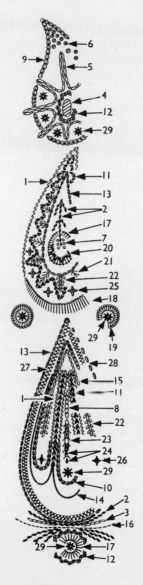

1 – 0280
2 – 0263 Stem Stitch
3 – 0386
4 – 0386 Satin Stitch
5 – 0386 Couching
6 – 0337 French Knots
7 – 0386
8 – 0337
9 – 0341 Chain Stitch
10 – 0280
11 – 0263
12 – 0280 Zig-Zag Chain Stitch
13 – 0341 Back Stitch
14 – 0263
15 – 0386 Back Stitch
16 – 0280
17 – 0337
18 – 0280 Buttonhole Stitch
19 – 0386
20 – 0263
21 – 0337 Fly Stitch
22 – 0386
23 – 0337 Wheatear Stitch
24 – 0263 Daisy Stitch
25 – 0337 Upright Cross Stitch
26 – 0263 with woven centre
27 – 0337 Herringbone Stitch
28 – 0341 Running Stitch
29 – 0263 Straight Stitch Stars

Suggestions for using the motifs

Suggestions for arrangement of motifs Motifs can be grouped together to form interesting patterns or strips for borders. Combinations of motifs can also give charming results.

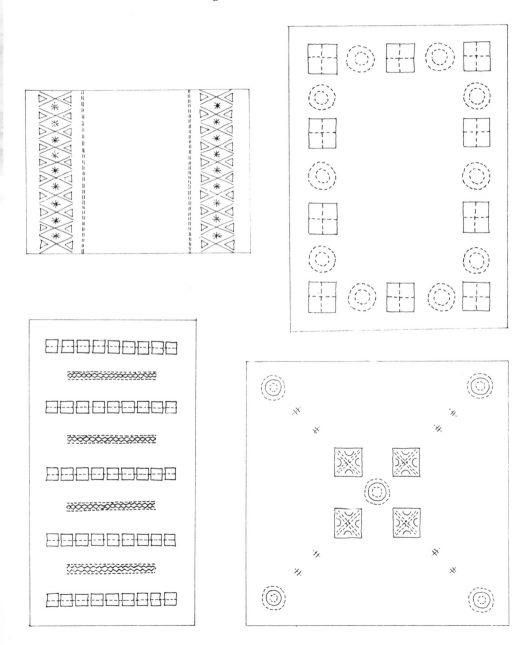

Index

A frock for a 4-year-old child, smocked and embroidered. A fine example of English folk embroidery.